# Biblically
# KOSHER

## A MESSIANIC JEWISH PERSPECTIVE ON KASHRUT

D1293403

# Biblically
# KOSHER

## A MESSIANIC JEWISH PERSPECTIVE ON KASHRUT

### REVEALING THE BIBLICAL SOURCES
### OF DIETARY LAWS IN JUDAISM

### AARON EBY

FIRST FRUITS OF
ZION

**First Edition 2012**
**Printed in the United States of America**

ISBN: 978-1-892124-61-6

Cover Design: Avner Wolff

Quantity discounts are available on bulk purchases of this book for educational, fundraising, or event purposes. Special versions or book excerpts to fit specific needs are available from First Fruits of Zion. For more information, contact www.ffoz.org/contact.

**First Fruits of Zion**

PO Box 649, Marshfield, Missouri 65706–0649 USA
Phone (417) 468–2741, www.ffoz.org

Comments and questions: www.ffoz.org/contact

# CONTENTS

# INTRODUCTION

K *ashrut* is the concept of dietary law in Judaism. It begins with the Bible's instructions about permitted ("kosher") food. Over the centuries, the Jewish community has applied, discussed, interpreted, and elaborated on these instructions, resulting in the system of laws and customs that exists today.

## The Place of Kashrut

The significance of *kashrut* stems from the centrality of food to life. People eat every day. Social events typically revolve around meals. Cultures are often distinguished by their cuisines.

Perhaps no greater factor affects human health more than the quality of food that we eat. The nutrients in food literally become our flesh and blood as well as the energy that animates them.

The mere sight or smell of food affects our thoughts. We involuntarily associate foods with our past experiences and memories. Tasty treats can effectively motivate desired behaviors.

Given the intensity of the sociological, physiological, and psychological connection humans have to food, one should not underestimate the spiritual aspect of what we eat. The very first prohibition recorded in the Bible was a dietary law (Genesis 2:16–17). Essentially, the fall of man resulted from a violation of *kashrut*.

Even the glimpses that the Scriptures give us into the future world involve eating. "I tell you, many will come from east and west and recline at table [that is, eat a meal] with Abraham, Isaac, and Jacob in the kingdom of heaven" (Matthew 8:11).

Kosher eating is also significant because of its intense connection with Jewish identity. Even people who know little about Judaism are often aware that observant Jews do not eat pork. Enemies of the Jewish people from the days of the Maccabees until the Spanish Inquisition have attempted to force Jews to eat non-kosher food as a disavowal of their Jewishness. This highlights how very symbolic our food choices are.

Nonetheless, one must understand the importance of *kashrut* in relation to the Torah's many other demands. *Kashrut* is one of several commandments that are very external in nature. Because of this, it becomes susceptible to misapplication. The holy and God-given commandments of *kashrut* can fall victim to our own pretentious hypocrisy.

One must remember that the Torah is much bigger than the few commandments that draw the most attention. Prominent observances like the Sabbath and holidays, wearing *tzitzit* (tassels) or *tefillin* (phylacteries), and eating kosher are the proverbial "tip of the iceberg"; the heart of Torah is deep beneath the surface.

To draw another analogy, these outward signs are like a national flag waving on the highest mast of a powerful ship. They serve an important role in defining and communicating identity, but they are merely an adornment of the main body of the Torah. It would be pointless and foolish to obsess over the flag's appearance while the sails are torn or the hull is corroded. This is what our Master Yeshua called "straining out a gnat and swallowing a camel" (Matthew 23:24).

Thus, to observe *kashrut* properly is to do so in a way that it becomes intertwined with other *mitzvot*. The boundaries and lessons it provides should inspire and equip a person to seek inner, essential holiness. *Kashrut* should go hand in hand with hospitality and generosity—providing food to the hungry, for example. Eating kosher should emerge from a heart of thankfulness, gentleness, and humility. As Yeshua said, "First clean the inside of the cup and the plate, that the outside also may be clean" (Matthew 23:26). However, note that he did not say, "Clean only the inside, for the outside does not matter."

The sages have noted the vicious cycle effect of godliness: "One *mitzvah* leads to another *mitzvah*" (m.*Avot* 4:2). This is one great reason to begin keeping kosher. But if *kashrut* does not lead one to improve in other areas of life, then that observance is superficial. Nonetheless, if one keeps kosher with the proper motivation and perspective, it has the power to transform his life and propel him into a more profound and intimate walk with the Creator.

## About This Book

This book was written from a Messianic Jewish perspective. It is intended for followers of Yeshua (Jesus of Nazareth) who want to understand the biblical sources at the core of dietary practices observed in Judaism today.

The standards and recommendations presented in this book are pertinent to Jewish individuals as well as to Gentiles who have made a personal decision to keep kosher. However, the Bible does not impose upon Gentiles all of the same dietary requirements to which Jews are bound. Gentiles do have some dietary requirements, which are explained in the section entitled "Kashrut for Gentiles." Additionally, this section offers several reasons why Gentile followers of Yeshua should feel encouraged to go beyond the bare minimum dietary standard.

This book is divided into three parts. In the first part, I present some of the reasons someone might keep kosher and the benefits of doing so, then I address passages in the New Testament that are often raised to argue that one need not or must not eat only kosher food. These are passages like, "Thus Jesus declared all foods clean" (Mark 7:19), "Let no one pass judgment on you in questions of food and drink" (Colossians 2:16), and, "Nothing is to be rejected if it is received with thanksgiving" (1 Timothy 4:4). The reader may be surprised to learn that these passages have little to say on the topic of *kashrut* at all.

The second part forms the core of the book. In this section, I present what the Torah says about *kashrut*. For each topic, we will examine the verses in their cultural, historical, and linguistic context in order to elucidate their plain meaning.

I originally wrote this section a few years ago to help people understand some of the personal decisions that I had made for my family. I wanted to show that many practices that people consider "rabbinic" and that appear to hang on thin air actually have valid sources in the Bible. As it turns out, eating "biblically kosher" is far more involved than simply avoiding pork and shellfish. Furthermore, even though I have limited this study of the kosher laws to what is directly revealed in the Bible, it would be a mistake to divorce the Torah of God from the people to whom he entrusted it—the Jewish people (see Romans 3:2).

My own experiences with striving to keep kosher in the context of a diverse community highlighted the need for the third section of the book. This section deals with the dynamics of keeping kosher in a Messianic community which includes both Jews and Gentiles with different forms of observance. It offers suggestions about how to balance, prioritize, and coordinate the complexities of community and convictions regarding food.

This book is not comprehensive. For the most part, this study still focuses on the theory of *kashrut* rather than on its practical details. For practical advice, the reader is advised to consult any of several books on the topic available from Jewish publishers or, better yet, attend a class on the subject. The information I provide here does not offer many firm conclusions, but provides a knowledge base that will help you make informed decisions about how you will approach this *mitzvah*.

Those who have read my original study will find that it has been revised and improved substantially in this book. Certain parts are more accurate, others are supported by better scholarship, and several sections of it are brand new. I extend my thanks to the many individuals who provided encouragement as well as feedback that helped improve the quality and effectiveness of this study.

# PART 1

# REASONS FOR KEEPING KOSHER

B efore we begin our analysis of biblical kosher laws, it would be appropriate to consider what purpose these laws serve and why God commanded them. Furthermore, what benefits are there to keeping kosher?

## Is Health the Reason for Kosher Laws?

Many people come to the conclusion that kosher laws were put in place in order to provide physical health benefits. Certain animals may be prone to disease or spoiling; they may be likely to contain toxic substances; or the human digestive system may not be capable of processing them. Although this is a thoughtful and reasonable hypothesis, the Bible does not offer this as rationale for the dietary laws.

In *The Laws of Kashrus*, Rabbi Binyomin Forst points out that Rambam expressed the idea that forbidden foods are not healthful. However, he notes that other Jewish scholars have rejected the idea that kosher laws are for health purposes:

> *Abarbanel* (*Vayikra* 11), argues that attributing the laws of *kashrus* to medicinal reasons, makes the Torah a mere medical text. This is obviously not the case as there are many poisonous herbs that are not prohibited by the Torah. If the purpose of *kashrus* is no more than a health issue, why were these herbs not included in its prohibitions? Furthermore, non-Jews who eat all the foods forbidden to us appear no less healthy than Jews who

abstain from these foods. A similar argument is made in *Sefer Akeidas Yitzchok* (60), which also strongly criticizes *Rambam's* view. If in fact the laws of *kashrus* were based on health, the Torah would not distinguish between Jew and non-Jew, as the Psalmist (145:9) declares "His mercies are on all His works." Why were the laws of *kashrus* not incorporated into the seven Noahide laws? *Abarbanel* notes the fact that the Torah uses the word *tamei* in regard to prohibited foods; the word "tamei" signifies spiritual defilement not physical harm. Obviously, *Abarbanel* concludes, the *mitzvos* are not intended to heal bodies and provide for their material welfare but to heal the soul and cure its illnesses.[1]

In reality, many foods that meet the Bible's kosher standards are unhealthy. For example, certain brands of sugary snack cakes and potato chips loaded with hydrogenated fats are fully kosher. Likewise, many highly nutritious dishes do not meet biblical dietary requirements. For example, rabbit farms often tout rabbit meat as "the most nutritious meat known to man" (citing a 1940 USDA circular) due to its low levels of fat and cholesterol and its high level of protein. Although the science of healthy eating constantly changes, biblical kosher law stays the same. There is not a direct relationship between kosher laws and nutrition.

This is also true for foods that are organically grown and raised. A pig or a cow raised on an organic farm is not any more or less kosher than one raised in an industrial environment, because the Bible does not make a distinction between what is organic and what is not. The distinction did not exist at the time the Bible was written. In certain circumstances, organic foods may be less likely to meet biblical kosher standards. For example, if an organic pesticide was less effective than a conventional one, it could result in a higher amount of bug-infested produce.

One who views kosher as synonymous with healthful might be tempted to disregard the biblical commandments in favor of what scientific studies determine to be the best diet. But this would be a mistake. Biblical scholar Dr. Nathan MacDonald recently published a book entitled *What Did the Ancient Israelites Eat? Diet in Bibli-*

*cal Times*, in which he makes the case that the diet of the ancient Israelites was not nutritious.

> Our current state of knowledge suggests that the population of Iron Age Israel generally suffered from an inadequate diet, poor health, and low life expectancy. Their experience was little different from that of other premodern inhabitants of Palestine, and in some respects it may even have been worse.[2]

People often assert that God gave the kosher laws to protect the Israelites from spoiled meat, diseases, and unsanitary practices. But in modern society, they reason, those are no longer of any concern. With modern refrigeration, disease prevention, and hygiene regulations, all foods should be permitted. But there are numerous problems with this assertion. First of all, it implies that kosher laws should not have been "abolished" in New Testament times, but only about a hundred years ago when modern sanitation and refrigeration methods began. Cows, sheep, goats, and chickens have also always been subject to spoiling and disease, just as pigs and camels are. Food produced even in first-world countries is still subject to health problems, as recent recalls due to *E. coli* and salmonella outbreaks prove. Furthermore, scientists still have much to learn about which foods cause health problems, as new studies are constantly published on the topic.

But most importantly, the Bible never claims that its food laws are for the purposes of health. After all, the very first dietary law in the Bible—the law against eating fruit from the tree of the knowledge of good and evil—was entirely spiritual in nature.

There are only a few justifications explicitly given in the Torah for the kosher laws: ritual purity, holiness, and sonship:

> For I am the LORD your God. Consecrate yourselves therefore, and be holy, for I am holy. You shall not defile yourselves with any swarming thing that crawls on the ground. For I am the LORD who brought you up out of the land of Egypt to be your God. You shall therefore be holy, for I am holy. This is the law about beast and bird and every living creature that moves through the waters and every creature that swarms on the ground, to make

a distinction between the unclean and the clean and between the living creature that may be eaten and the living creature that may not be eaten. (Leviticus 11:44–47)

You are the sons of the LORD your God. You shall not cut yourselves or make any baldness on your foreheads for the dead. For you are a people holy to the LORD your God, and the LORD has chosen you to be a people for his treasured possession, out of all the peoples who are on the face of the earth. You shall not eat any abomination. (Deuteronomy 14:1–3)

It is noteworthy that none of these reasons relate to health. To the contrary, they seem to be related to our spiritual condition and our relationship with God.

For Jews, the ultimate reason for keeping kosher is to maintain covenant fidelity. God made a covenant with the Jewish people. As a part of that covenant, he revealed the Torah and the commandments. Some of those commandments concern what is or is not to be eaten. Keeping kosher means being loyal to the God who created you, knows you, chose you, and loves you.

There are also good reasons for Gentiles to take on kosher laws as well. In addition to the spiritual benefits listed below, see the discussion of Gentiles and *kashrut* in part three of this book.

## Spiritual Benefits of Keeping Kosher

While we have established that we cannot know exactly why God gave dietary laws, we can perceive that there are *benefits* to keeping kosher.

### Discipline and Self Control

An essential part of being human is our constant struggle between our animalistic nature and our spiritual nature. In the Bible, these aspects are often termed "the flesh" and "the spirit." Yeshua remarked, "The spirit indeed is willing, but the flesh is weak" (Matthew 26:41; Mark 14:38). Paul frequently speaks of the conflict between the spirit and the flesh (for example, see Romans 8). In Judaism today, these same concepts are typically referred to as "the evil inclination" (*yetzer hara*, יֵצֶר הָרַע) and "the good inclination" (*yetzer hatov*, יֵצֶר הַטּוֹב). If a person's spiritual nature does not master his physical desires, he behaves no differently from an animal.

Eating is one of the most primal of human desires. Learning to control one's desires is essential to spiritual life. If one cannot control something as basic as what enters his mouth, how can he hope to control more advanced and abstract aspects of his life? Likewise, one whose diet is governed by his spiritual discipline is accustomed to saying "no" to his primal desires. He will have greater capacity to withstand the temptation to steal from or exploit others, commit sexual sins, or harm other people.

Keeping a kosher diet can help a person to be constantly aware of God's presence. A person who keeps kosher lives consciously and purposefully. His or her choices about food are intentional and reflect a posture of service toward the Creator.

## Holiness and Purity

The Torah's instructions about the food laws emphasize purity and holiness. Animals forbidden for food are called *tamei* (טָמֵא), which can be translated "impure" or "unclean." The food laws are given along with the explanation that God's people are to be holy.

Purity, as it is expressed in the Torah, is a type of distance from the corrupt and mortal condition of the world. Sources of impurity in the Torah relate to death. Predatory animals such as lions, bears, wolves, sharks, and birds of prey are inherently *tamei* and not kosher. The same is true for scavengers. In contrast, the animals fit for sacrificial purposes are cattle, sheep, and goats. Not only do these animals graze peacefully on plant matter; as domesticated livestock they are even removed from the natural predatory cycle of the wild.

Purity is a step toward holiness. The essence of holiness is distinction, since to be holy is to be set apart, distinguished, or designated for a spiritual or divine purpose. Through the dietary laws, the ancient Israelites were made distinct from the surrounding Canaanite cultures. To this day, archaeologists who uncover ancient ruins are able to identify Israelite settlements by virtue of the lack of pig bones. Likewise, modern observant Jews are made distinct from general society by keeping kosher.

The type of holiness achieved through *kashrut* is an external and physical one. It absolutely must be accompanied by purity and holiness in other aspects of life, such as thoughts, words, and behaviors. But it is nonetheless important. It is spiritual simply because it is an act of submission to God's will, and it can lead to other spiritual behaviors as well.

Keeping kosher affects one's lifestyle. It sometimes dictates where a person can go, what a person can do, or how far one can distance himself from his spiritual community. Just as food helped to shield the ancient Israelites from idolatry, it can help preserve people today from surrounding themselves with godlessness and destructive spiritual environments.

One *mitzvah* can lead to another *mitzvah*. By submitting to God by keeping a kosher diet, a person paves the way for other improvements in his or her spiritual life.

## Spirituality and Morality

Keeping kosher has the potential to enhance a person's spirituality and sense of morality. Each aspect of kosher law can remind us of proper behaviors and character.

For example, kosher land animals which graze for food can be seen to symbolize peace and gentleness. They do not sustain their own lives by taking life from others as predators do.

Split hooves and rumination, the two signs of kosher land animals, can be seen as representing both external and internal purity. A pig is particularly objectionable because it appears to be kosher on the outside, but internally it is not. From *kashrut* we also learn lessons about compassion, kindness, family life, patience, and holiness.

When our master Yeshua met the Gadarene demoniacs (Matthew 8:28–34), why is it that the demons begged to be cast into pigs? We can only speculate, but it may very well be the case that there is something spiritually unhealthy about that particular species, something that cannot possibly be known or detected by science.

What we eat literally becomes a part of us—it is integrated into our physical bodies and is converted into the energy that moves us. Could the food we eat also have a spiritual effect on us?

Every living animal eats; only humans have the presence of mind to rise above our instincts and make choices about what we eat. Eating is one of the most mundane activities humans perform, but we have the capacity to transform the activity into an act of worship and holiness. By choosing to keep kosher, one decides not to let his physical body and its desires govern his life.

## The Importance of Keeping Kosher for Messianic Jews

Maintaining Jewish identity is one of the greatest challenges the Jewish community has had to face. The rate of assimilation is a constant threat to the survival of Judaism. The solution is to instill in Jewish children a sense that their Jewish identity is significant and something to be proud of. They need to be connected with their heritage and their people. They need to find meaning in their practice of Judaism and feel a sense of continuity with their ancestors.

Given that Jewish identity in general is under such a substantial threat, it stands to reason that Messianic Jewish identity is even more endangered. Messianic Jews are far fewer in number. Our communities are more scattered and fragmented. We lack educated leaders and access to resources. We tend to be held at arm's length from the rest of the Jewish community. Many Messianic Jews feel a sense of estrangement from the Jewish community due to past experiences. Others have theological antagonism toward mainstream Judaism. Furthermore, our dual identity as both Jews and followers of Yeshua can leave us in no-man's land. While it is important to maintain positive interaction with the Christian world at large, this also exposes us and our children to the risk of losing our sense of Jewishness. All of this leaves our precious community as fragile as a particle of antimatter in a containment field.

It is an ironic tragedy that Messianic Jews are commonly so estranged from Judaism. As followers of the Messiah, our community should be leading the way in covenant faithfulness and Jewish identity. Messianic Jewish scholar Dr. Mark Kinzer observes,

> … according to New Testament teaching, the ekklesia contains at its core a portion of Israel. Paul calls this por-

tion "the remnant" and describes it as a representative and priestly component of Israel that sanctifies Israel as a whole. In order to fulfill its vocation, this portion of Israel must truly *live as Israel*—that is, it must be exemplary in observing those traditional Jewish practices that identify the Jewish people as a distinct community chosen and loved by God.[3]

If the fledgling modern Messianic Jewish movement is to survive into the next generation, there will need to be a strong push toward legitimate Jewish observance. Beyond any theological or spiritual argument we might make, our *sociological* need for Jewish practice is intense. We must have something tangible that forges a connection between our children and the Jewish community as a whole.

D. Thomas Lancaster writes,

Hundreds, thousands, tens of thousands, and hundreds of thousands of Jewish people have come to faith in Messiah and have become Christians over the last century and a half, but they are almost all gone—vanished. Over the last two thousand years, a steady stream of Jewish people has confessed Messiah, beginning with the generation of the apostles, but they are gone, too, like chaff in the wind. They have left no enduring legacy. There is no Jewish form of Christianity or ongoing Jewish legacy of faith in Yeshua because, as soon as the Jewish people become believers, they are taught, "Now that you are a Christian, there is no difference between you and us, and you may marry our children, and our children may marry yours, and you no longer need to be Jewish or keep kosher, or keep Sabbath, or do anything that would preserve your identity as a Jew. You are no longer under the law."[4]

Education in Jewish literacy is important, but it is not enough. Simply telling children that they are Jewish does little to solidify their identity. Using Jewish symbols and terminology is superficial without actual practice backing it up. Children need to be shown and not merely told.

*Kashrut* is one of the most basic aspects of Jewish observance. It has unique power to reinforce and preserve Jewish identity:

1. Since social activities often revolve around food, one's diet can determine which social groups a person can join. For children especially, the distinction forged by their special diet can solidify and reinforce their identity and help prevent assimilation in other areas.

2. A person who keeps kosher will need to live in an area where kosher food is readily available. Most likely, this means living in an area near other Jews. This will further strengthen Jewish identity and enable further participation in the Jewish community and Jewish events.

3. If keeping kosher is important to a person, then they will also need to find a spouse with the same conviction. A spouse who keeps kosher will be more likely to feel close to his or her Jewish identity. As a result, Jewishness will be a key component of their family life.

Reform Judaism has struggled to redefine aspects of Torah observance. To Reform Jews, *kashrut* often has less to do with forbidden species and more to do with environmentalism, treatment of animals, social concerns, and health. And yet it is impossible to escape the idea that *kashrut* is essential to Jewish identity. Peter Knobel, a Reform-affiliated Jewish writer, shares his experience:

> Central to the ability of any particular form of kashrut to serve as a part of Jewish identity formation is that it must on a conscious or unconscious level connect one to other Jews. About thirty years ago, I was engaged with some congregants in an informal study session on Yom Kippur afternoon. Someone asked me about my own level of kashrut. Having grown up in a classical Reform environment, I did not keep any form of kashrut at that time. Then, one woman, a Holocaust survivor, said to me. "You eat the flesh of the swine?" The answer was, of course, "Yes." That was a revelatory moment. I realized that I needed a dietary practice that reminded me every time I sat down to eat that I was Jewish. As a result, I gave

up all pork products, not because I did not like them. In fact, a serious foodie, I miss eating them to this very day, but refraining from eating pork immediately identified me with the Jewish people. It reminded me that in times of persecution, anti-Semites often tried to humiliate Jews by making them eat forbidden foods, especially pork. Yet, in times of extremis (e.g., the Shoah), some Jews, even when starving, refused to eat forbidden foods as a sign of loyalty to the covenant and resistance to persecution. Refraining from pork has had a powerful affect [sic] on my identity as a Jew.[5]

In the past few decades, any semblance of keeping kosher in the Messianic Jewish movement has been largely for evangelistic purposes. We could call this "missionary *kashrut*." People involved in Jewish evangelism often find that their testimony falls on deaf ears if they admit to eating overtly prohibited foods such as pork. To prevent food from being a stumbling block to the gospel, they abstain from pork and perhaps shellfish.

At the very least, this should highlight the intense connection between Jewish identity and *kashrut*. Jews who are targeted by evangelism efforts instinctively know that if Jesus abolished the dietary laws, then he was like so many false prophets and antagonists who have tried to destroy Israel. As Dr. Kinzer puts it,

> *The abolition of the dietary laws is in effect an abolition of the Jewish people itself.* Like circumcision and holiday observance, the Torah's dietary regimen serves as a fundamental sign of the particular vocation and identity of the Jewish people.[6]

It is true that when Jews who profess Yeshua fail to keep kosher, they reflect very negatively on him. And yet, missionary *kashrut* is not enough to sustain the Messianic Jewish movement. For observance of *kashrut* to have its needed effect, it needs to arise from the desire of Messianic Jews to carry out their covenant obligations and divine mission as Jews.

# OBJECTIONS TO KEEPING KOSHER

It might seem simple to say, "Jesus fulfilled the Law, and therefore it is not necessary to keep kosher." But there are many problems with this view.

## Can Kosher Law Be Overturned?

### The Least in the Kingdom

The statement that Yeshua "fulfilled the Law" comes from Matthew 5:

> Do not think that I have come to abolish the Law or the Prophets; I have not come to abolish them but to fulfill them. For truly, I say to you, until heaven and earth pass away, not an iota, not a dot, will pass from the Law until all is accomplished. Therefore whoever relaxes one of the least of these commandments and teaches others to do the same will be called least in the kingdom of heaven, but whoever does them and teaches them will be called great in the kingdom of heaven. For I tell you, unless your righteousness exceeds that of the scribes and Pharisees, you will never enter the kingdom of heaven (Matthew 5:17–20).

From this we can see that "fulfilling" the Torah cannot mean putting it to an end. If Yeshua taught people to relax or neglect the dietary laws in the Torah, he would be called "least in the kingdom of heaven" according to his own words. We cannot say that "all is accomplished" because Yeshua defines this as "until heaven and earth pass away."

To understand Yeshua's statement that he has come to "fulfill" the Torah, one must be familiar with the Hebraic terminology that he used. In Judaism, to "fulfill" the Torah means to uphold it—that is to say, to treat it with importance and carry out its commandments. In contrast, to "abolish" the Torah means the opposite: to disregard or violate the commandments.[7]

"Fulfilling" the Torah in the sense of putting it to an end is a concept foreign to Judaism, because the Torah is not a problem waiting to be solved. Likewise, if a citizen of the United States keeps all of the laws established by the government, he does not free other people from doing so.

That means that if Yeshua "fulfilled" the Torah's kosher laws, it simply means that he kept and upheld them. But if he put them to an end, he would be the "least in the kingdom."

## The False Prophet

God explicitly instructed the Jewish people to reject any so-called prophet who enticed them to stray from the commandments, even if they performed miraculous signs to prove their authority. If Yeshua, Paul, or anyone else spoke against the food laws, he would match Moses' description of a false prophet.

> If a prophet or a dreamer of dreams arises among you and gives you a sign or a wonder, and the sign or wonder that he tells you comes to pass, and if he says, 'Let us go after other gods,' which you have not known, 'and let us serve them,' you shall not listen to the words of that prophet or that dreamer of dreams. For the LORD your God is testing you, to know whether you love the LORD your God with all your heart and with all your soul. You shall walk after the LORD your God and fear him and keep his commandments and obey his voice, and you shall serve him and hold fast to him. But that prophet or that dreamer of dreams shall be put to death, because he has taught rebellion against the LORD your God, who brought you out of the land of Egypt and redeemed you out of the house of slavery, to make you leave the way in which the

LORD your God commanded you to walk. So you shall purge the evil from your midst. (Deuteronomy 13:1–5)

We can be confident that Yeshua kept all of the kosher laws of the Bible. If he had not, he would be a sinner, since disobeying the laws of the Torah is sin by definition.[8] If he was a sinner, he certainly could not have been the Messiah. But the Bible assures us that he was sinless (Hebrews 4:15, 7:26; 1 Peter 2:22; 2 Corinthians 5:21).

All of the biblical prophets urged the Jewish people in the strongest possible terms to keep the commandments, including the kosher laws.[9] Yeshua, as the ultimate prophet and king of Israel, would have to uphold, observe, and teach all of the laws. As Ezekiel foretells concerning the Messiah:

> My servant David shall be king over them, and they shall all have one shepherd. They shall walk in my rules and be careful to obey my statutes. (Ezekiel 37:24)

If Yeshua had taught against the dietary laws in the Torah, he would not qualify as a prophet or the Messiah.

### The Jerusalem Council

In Acts 15, the apostles were presented with the question of whether or not Gentiles who were turning to God must become Jewish through a conversion process and keep the entire Torah. One might think that the answer to this question should be obvious, yet to the apostles this was a very difficult matter. It was only after "there had been much debate" (Acts 15:7) that Peter made his final point and the question was settled.

When the apostles listed their directives to Gentiles, they did not tell them that they were free from all dietary obligations. Rather, the apostles instructed them to abstain from "the things polluted by idols, and from sexual immorality, and from what has been strangled, and from blood" (Acts 15:20).

Remember, the question at hand was whether *Gentiles* must keep the Torah. This question would not even have been raised if it was not already clear that Jews should do so. If even Gentiles are instructed to abide by these parameters, it stands to reason that Jews also have dietary parameters to live by—the Torah's food laws.

If other passages in the New Testament seem to imply that there are absolutely no parameters for food whatsoever, then they stand in contradiction to this passage. Granted, the apostles do not decree here that pork, for instance, is off-limits for Gentiles, but they do make it clear that there are some things that Gentiles cannot eat.

Therefore, when we read statements in the New Testament such as "Jesus declared all foods clean," "Nothing is to be rejected," or, "Nothing is unclean in itself," we must either accept that they contradict the apostolic decree or that they refer to something other than elimination of all dietary restrictions. As this study will show, many of these passages are not speaking about the kosher laws at all.

### Summary: Can Kosher Law Be Overturned?

As we have seen, the claim that "Jesus fulfilled the law" is not enough to argue against keeping kosher for multiple reasons:

> Yeshua explicitly upheld the enduring validity of the entire Torah and condemned those who taught otherwise. This includes the dietary commandments.

> If Yeshua had attempted to instruct others to neglect *kashrut* or any other commandment, then he would meet the biblical definition of a false prophet and would not qualify as the Messiah.

> The apostles decreed that even Gentiles have some dietary obligations. How much more so, then, for Jews!

These points call into question the traditional interpretation of several New Testament passages which are commonly invoked to refute keeping kosher. These passages must be understood in the proper cultural, historical, linguistic, and religious context.

# Holiness, Purity, and Kashrut: Mark 7 and Acts 10

To grasp the meaning many of the New Testament's teachings, it is essential to understand what holiness, purity, and kosher status meant in the context of Second Temple Judaism. These concepts began with biblical law (predominantly the book of Leviticus), but over time additional nuances, customs, and laws were added. Purity laws were especially important to the Pharisees, who appear prominently in the Gospel narratives. Without understanding the way these concepts are used in Leviticus and later applied in Jewish law, it is easy to misunderstand critical passages in the New Testament.

**Holiness** : An object might be "holy" or "non-holy." Another way to phrase this is "consecrated" or "non-consecrated." This is not a moral status but a matter of dedication. For example, an animal might be dedicated as a sacrifice in the Temple. By virtue of that dedication, the animal becomes consecrated or holy. After the animal is slaughtered in the Temple grounds, a portion is burned on the altar, and the remainder is given to the priests to eat. The meat from this sacrifice is also consecrated or holy. As a consequence, it can only be eaten by certain people under certain conditions. The Hebrew word for "holy" is *kadosh* (קָדוֹשׁ). As a noun, a consecrated offering is called *kodesh* (קֹדֶשׁ), and the plural is *kodashim* (קָדָשִׁים). Food that is not dedicated in such a manner is *chol* (חֹל), an adjective or noun, the plural of which is *chullin* (חוּלִין). Although *chol* is the opposite of *kadosh*, there is no negative association with non-holiness. Any ordinary food is *chullin*. It is not a sin to eat *chullin*; in fact, it is perfectly normal and acceptable.

However, holiness is used in a broader sense as well. *Kadosh* can be defined as "set apart, distinguished, or designated for a spiritual or divine purpose." Holiness is a matter of degree; certain things are more holy than others. The more something is dedicated and bears uniqueness pertaining to its spiritual purpose, the more holy it is.

A type of holiness can be achieved externally through ritual means. For example, the high priest of Israel, regardless of his moral character, has a degree of holiness simply by being designated in his position.

When referring to humans, there is another aspect of holiness that is internal or essential. This is something accomplished through engaging in behaviors that are spiritually elevating and abstaining from those that are not. These godly behaviors create distinctiveness and uniqueness, a process called "sanctification." For example, Peter cites the Torah's commands of holiness, saying, "As obedient children, do not be conformed to the passions of your former ignorance, but as he who called you is holy, you also be holy in all your conduct, since it is written, 'You shall be holy, for I am holy'" (1 Peter 1:14–16, citing Leviticus 11:44, 19:2, 20:7).

**Purity** : An object might be pure or impure. This is a legally defined ritual state unrelated to hygiene. "Pure" in Hebrew is *tahor* (טָהוֹר), and "impure" is *tamei* (טָמֵא). People, food, and other objects might be *tahor* or *tamei*. Like *kadosh* and *chol*, there is no moral problem with being *tamei*, as it is a common, natural state. There is also no prohibition against eating food that is *tamei*. For example, if a person comes in contact with a corpse (perhaps in the process of burying a deceased relative), he not only becomes *tamei* himself, but he also causes things to become *tamei* by touching them.[10] This lasts for seven days. Everything he eats for that period of time will inevitably be *tamei*.

However, it is important not to contaminate something that is *kadosh* (consecrated) by making it *tamei*. That means that a person who is *tamei* must become purified before he can enter the sacred Temple precincts or eat meat from a sacrifice.[11]

**Acceptability** : Food can either be permitted or forbidden. Food that is acceptable for eating is called *kasher* (כָּשֵׁר). English speakers may be more familiar with the Ashkenazi (Eastern European) pronunciation *kosher*. The relationship between acceptability, purity, and holiness is complex.

Some species of animals (namely those listed as such in Leviticus 11 and Deuteronomy 14) are intrinsically *tamei* (impure). Along with being *tamei*, they are also unacceptable (non-kosher) for food. But that does not mean that everything that is *tamei* is not kosher. A cow is an intrinsically *tahor* animal, but if a person who was contaminated by a corpse touches a kosher slice of beef, it becomes *tamei* while remaining kosher. An animal of an intrinsically kosher and *tahor* species can become non-kosher and *tamei* if it is not properly slaughtered but dies of natural causes.[12]

Furthermore, even food that is holy can become non-kosher. For example, to a person that is *tamei*, holy foods are not permissible and are therefore non-kosher, although they may be kosher to someone else. An animal that is consecrated as an offering but then is disqualified due to a blemish is also holy but not kosher. Certain foods may only be eaten by priests; to the typical Israelite, the food is not kosher.

Today, foods can be kosher or non-kosher, but the notions of holiness and purity in the sense described above are mere thought exercises, since there is no Temple through which anything can be consecrated or purified. In the days of the Gospels, these issues were quite tangible and relevant to daily life.

Here is a summary of the terms described above:

| Term | Meaning | Opposite | Meaning |
|------|---------|----------|---------|
| *kadosh* | holy/consecrated | *chol* | common |
| *tahor* | pure | *tamei* | impure |
| *kasher* | acceptable | *lo kasher* | unacceptable |

## Jesus Declared All Foods Clean

Mark 7 relates a story of an encounter between Yeshua's disciples and some critical Pharisees. In the course of this encounter, the narrator of the Gospel inserts a parenthetical statement: "[Yeshua] declared all foods clean" (Mark 7:19). One might interpret this statement to mean that kosher laws no longer apply. In fact, the New Living Translation takes the liberty of interpreting the verse "By saying this, he declared that every kind of food is acceptable in God's eyes."

But this interpretation raises some serious problems. In addition to the objections noted in the section "Can Kosher Law Be Overturned?" we can raise two more objections that specifically relate to this passage.

First, when Yeshua's disciple Peter beheld the vision of the sheet recorded in Acts (discussed below), Peter was shocked by the notion of eating non-kosher animals and insisted that he had "never eaten anything that is common or unclean" (Acts 10:14). If Yeshua had changed the dietary laws in Mark 7, then Peter must have been unaware of it, or his vision was unnecessary.

Second, Yeshua criticized the Pharisees in this passage for "rejecting the commandment of God" (Mark 7:9) and "making void the word of God" (Mark 7:13). If Yeshua invalidated the God-given dietary laws at the same time that he leveled this harsh criticism, he would be guilty of hypocrisy and his argument would fall flat.

How, then, are we to understand and apply Yeshua's complete argument and the verse in question?

## The Accusation

The ESV's translation describes the offenders' hands as "defiled" and speaks about what "defiles" a person. Earlier, we discussed the different but interrelated concepts of consecrated/common, pure/impure, and kosher/not kosher. Which of these concepts corresponds with the term "defiled"?

"Kosher" and "not kosher" (in this context) are concepts that only apply to food. The question here is not about the food (bread) that they ate, but the people and their hands.

Since the text speaks about hand washing, we may naturally assume that we are dealing with the concepts of pure (*tahor*) and impure (*tamei*). After all, the purpose of ceremonial hand washing is to remove impurity (*tum'ah*) from the hands. Most translations of Mark into Hebrew follow this cue and use the term *tamei*.

The Greek word translated as "defiled" is *koinos* (κοινός), which means "common" and is often used in a sense that means "together" or "in general." For example, the word is used to describe the believers who "had all things in common" (Acts 2:44). From a semantic perspective, it seems that *koinos* corresponds more directly with the Hebrew term *chol* (common), rather than *tamei* (impure).

In contrast, the Greek word that the Septuagint uses to translate *tamei* is *akathartos* (ἀκάθαρτος). It literally means "impure" and it is the opposite of *katharos* (καθαρός), which means "pure." The term *akathartos* does not appear in this passage at all.

It is not unheard of for *koinos* to describe something *tamei*.[13] But this less precise choice of words suggests that the topic of dispute is not a matter of ritual purity *per se* but of holiness. When Yeshua declared that "things that come out of a person are what defile him," he taught that they compromise a person's holiness.

This makes sense because, for the Pharisees, ritual purity was not an end in itself but a method for achieving holiness. Yeshua's words communicated that holiness was a moral and ethical matter, not only a ritual condition.

## Purifying All Foods

> And he said to them, "Then are you also without under-standing? Do you not see that whatever goes into a person from outside cannot defile him, since it enters not his heart but his stomach, and is expelled [into the toilet]?" (Thus he declared all foods clean.) And he said, "What comes out of a person is what defiles him. For from within, out of the heart of man, come evil thoughts, sexual immorality, theft, murder, adultery, coveting, wicked-ness, deceit, sensuality, envy, slander, pride, foolishness. All these evil things come from within, and they defile a person." (Mark 7:18–23)

The ESV presumably left out the words "into the toilet" (*eis ton afedrona*, εἰς τὸν ἀφεδρῶνα) to prevent back-pew snickering.

In addition to the objections raised at the beginning of this chapter, we can note additional difficulties. If the declaration that all foods are now permitted is based on the realization that food passes through the digestive system, then there was no basis for God to give food laws in the first place. After all, nothing changed about the human body when Yeshua came. Furthermore, if it is based on his concluding statement about unethical and immoral behaviors, then again there is no basis for a change, since these have been prohibited all along as well.

The Greek text translated "Thus he declared all foods clean" is as follows:

| καθαρίζων | πάντα | τὰ | βρώματα |
|---|---|---|---|
| *katharizon* | *panta* | *ta* | *bromata* |
| purifying | all | the | foods |

*Katharizon* (καθαρίζων) is from the verb *katharizo* (καθαρίζω), which means "purify," "cleanse," or "make clean."

The term *katharizon* is a participle in the present tense, as in "purifying." It is masculine in gender, but there is no explicit subject. This leads translators to ask: who or what is doing the purifying in this verse? In order to find a word that will provide a subject that makes any sense and matches grammatically, one must go all the way back to "he said" (*legei*, λέγει)[14] in the beginning of 7:18. This would mean that Yeshua (the one who "said") is the one doing the purifying of the foods.

The word "declare" is not explicit in Greek; translators see it as implied in the word *katharizon*, since if Yeshua is the one purifying, he is doing so by his words. Most of the time *katharizo* and the Hebrew equivalent *tihar* (טָהַר) refers to physical purification such as through a process of washing. However, in the case of a *metzora* (commonly, "leper") who exhibits signs of purity, the priest "purifies" him—that is to say, pronounces him pure. (In Rabbinic literature, the term can also mean "to legally determine something to be pure.")

This is the justification for most translators' decision to elaborate on the verse, adding words like, "By saying this, Jesus declared …" none of which are explicit in Greek.

However, the grammar in this verse is difficult. Sure, *legei* ("he said") provides a subject for *katharizon* ("purifying"), but the distance between those two words is problematic. The grammatical principles would apply more naturally if it had been written:

> And **he said** to them, "*All foods are hereby purified,*" **purifying** all foods.

Instead, we have:

> And **he said** to them, "*Then are you also without understanding? Do you not see that whatever goes into a person from outside cannot defile him, since it enters not his heart but his stomach, and is expelled into the toilet?*" **purifying** all foods.

Not only is the separation a problem, but simply stating something that has always been true—which in fact the listener should already have known—does not purify anything. It is not analogous to a priest pronouncing a former *metzora* pure, nor is it similar to a rabbi's declaration that a questionable item is *tahor*.

## Purging All Meats

The mainstay of pro-Torah interpretation of this verse has been to rely on the Textus Receptus that forms the basis of the King James Version. It contains a slight textual variant that changes the gender of the word *katharizon* from masculine (καθαρίζων) to neuter (καθαρίζον). In this case, "purifying" does not line up with "he," but seems to describe the digestive process in general:

> Because it entereth not into his heart, but into the belly, and goeth out into the draught, purging all meats? (Mark 7:19, KJV)

From this perspective, the end of the verse is not a parenthetical statement inserted by the narrator, but a part of what Yeshua said to make his point: the food is "purged," that is, "eliminated" from the body.

The above reading would solve all of the difficulties raised thus far. The text (and Yeshua's argument) would flow smoothly and coherently. There would be no third-party commentator intruding on the text with a non sequitur.

However, this interpretation has flaws. The masculine form is much more likely to be original, since it is found in the oldest and most reliable manuscripts. Nonetheless, the change highlights the difficulty in the grammar, as scribes would sometimes smooth over what they perceived as errors in the text.

An additional problem with this interpretation is that the word "foods" (*ta bromata*) is still the object of *katharizon*. In other words, it does not say "purifying the body" but "purifying the food."

## Dangling Participles

The Gospel of Mark is not written in refined Greek. As John Painter writes, "Limited facility with syntax, grammar and vocabulary makes clear that Mark is not a work of 'high literature' and was capable of being read by those of moderate education."[15] Ben Witherington explains that "Matthew and Luke deliberately smooth out the harsh, rough edges of Mark's grammar and syntax and vocabulary … Mark's Greek is not elegant and his rhetoric not advanced."[16] The awkwardness and grammatical errors in the Marcan text are possibly due to its narrative style and closeness to the oral sources. Some scholars also attribute this to its underlying Hebraic thought patterns.[17]

Grammar is not always a gateway to meaning. For example, suppose your friend told you the following:

> After shopping for groceries all day long, our refrigerator was full of food.

Most people would probably not even notice the grammatical error, especially if it was said aloud. It is normal for spoken language to contain grammatical errors.

But a person studying English as a second language might puzzle over this statement. The word "shopping" is a participle. But who or what was the one "shopping"? The participle should be construed with a nominative noun. The only nominative noun in the sentence is "refrigerator." From the grammar of this sentence, one could insist that the refrigerator spent all day shopping for groceries, which of course is ridiculous. The statement contains a grammatical error, but it is forgivable and, to natural readers, it still gets the point across.

Our verse in Mark contains a similar grammatical situation. One can insist that "purifying" has to be construed with "he said," but in addition to being strained by the distance of two complete sentences, the resulting interpretation is nonsensical. But if Yeshua is not the one "purifying," then who or what is?

## Koshering All Foods?

Before exploring other possibilities of the subject of the participle, a few more details should be added.

Nowhere in this entire passage (prior to 7:19) is the topic of *kashrut* (dietary law) mentioned. The only topics it discusses are ritual purity and holiness. The only food it specifically mentions is bread (7:5), although the ESV leaves it untranslated, probably since "bread" is often an idiom for food in general. However, the mention of bread is significant in this case, since it is one of the few types of *chullin* for which Jewish law requires washing.

*Katharizon* means "purifying," that is, "making *tahor*." Since neither the Torah nor Jewish law insists that the food that Jews

# Technical Note: Grammatical Errors in Mark?

Some folks might be surprised or disturbed by the idea that grammatical errors could appear in the Greek New Testament. However, scholars of Biblical Greek are well aware of the Bible's many "solecisms." These need not be viewed as a challenge to faith; rather, they are evidence that real human beings witnessed and recorded the events. Furthermore, they attest to the strength of the textual tradition by showing that most copyists preserved the words faithfully, even in cases where the Greek was not perfect.

For another example of a similar grammatical error in the Gospel of Mark, we can look at Mark 12:38–40. There Yeshua warns, "Beware of the scribes." The word for "scribes" is *grammateon* (γραμματέων), a plural, masculine noun in the genitive case.

According to the rules of Greek grammar, participles that describe the scribes should agree with *grammateon*: plural, masculine, and genitive. The first participle that follows is "like" — the Greek word *thelonton* (θελόντων), which does agree; it is plural, masculine, and genitive. The next participle is "devour" — the Greek word *katesthiontes* (κατεσθίοντες). This does not quite agree; it is plural and masculine, but it is nominative instead of genitive.

The Gospel of Luke relates the same saying of Yeshua (Luke 20:46–47). The basic text in Luke's version is word-for-word the same, but there are a few simple changes that make the text smoother. One change is that instead of using a participle for "devour," he switched it to an indicative verb so that it agrees with "scribes" and reads clearer. In other words, Luke corrected Mark's grammatical mistake.

There are no nominative or genitive cases in Hebrew or Aramaic, so if Yeshua's original statement was in one of those languages, it could not have had that grammatical problem. It would only have occurred when someone attempted to translate his words into Greek.

eat must be *tahor* (pure),[18] this has no effect on its kosher status. One might presume that *katharizon* is meant as "koshering" or "making kosher," but since *kashrut* has not been mentioned, this is a step too far.

But did all foods become *tahor* by Yeshua's statement? This would be just as problematic, since purity is also a matter of Torah law that cannot be abolished.

The phrase translated "all foods" is *panta ta bromata*. The word *ta* is the definite article ("the"). This phrase might describe all foods everywhere for all time, or it could describe "all of *the* foods," that is, the food described earlier as "whatever goes into a person." The word translated "whatever" is also *pan*, literally "all." If we interpret it this way, it would mean "purifying all of the foods [that the person ate]." But how would the food that a person ate become *tahor*?

### Purely Repulsive

While ritual purity is the central issue of this pericope, it is one of the most difficult concepts for interpreters to understand. Our minds make natural associations between ritual impurity and things that are dirty or gross. However, ritual impurity is legally defined and does not correlate with hygiene.

The Torah associates impurity with a very specific set of causes: blood lost in childbirth, carcasses, menstruation, semen, and *tzara'at* ("leprosy"). These items all have to do with the cycle of life and death.

Although it may seem counterintuitive, other types of repugnant or unpleasant substances are not inherently *tamei*. Digestive excrement, not being directly connected with life and death, is not considered *tamei*, even if it comes from an inherently *tamei* animal.[19] However, it is considered repulsive and as such is subject to a certain set of laws of its own. Deuteronomy 23:12–14 explains that the elimination of waste should occur outside the camp— not because it is *tamei*, but because it is *ervat davar* (עֶרְוַת דָּבָר), "something distasteful" or "something indecent." Based on this idea, Jewish law prohibits prayer in the presence of waste matter or unpleasant smells.

Dung, in fact, is treated in Jewish law like stone in that it *cannot* contract ritual impurity. The Mishnah (m.*Kelim* 10:1) lists dung among materials that can be used to make a vessel that will protect its contents from impurity.

Since dung has this quality, the Gemara (b.*Menachot* 69a–b) raises some hypothetical questions:

- Is grain found in animal droppings legally considered "dung," making it unable to contract impurity? (They concluded that once it is removed from the dung and intended for use as food, it is again susceptible.)

- Suppose an elephant eats a basket that was once *tamei*, and then it comes out in his waste, retaining its shape. Would the basket now be considered "dung," making it *tahor* and unsusceptible to impurity? (They concluded that since it did not change its form, it retains its original status.)

- Suppose an elephant just eats some twigs, and they happen to come out in a basket-like shape? Can this "basket" contract impurity since it has changed its form?

To investigate this last question, the sages appeal to a disturbing but legally relevant episode. During a famine, a wolf once ate two children.[20] A human corpse is not only *tamei*, but it transmits impurity to anything it touches. Since the wolf's droppings contain human remains, would they be *tahor* (being dung) or would they retain their status as human remains and transmit impurity? (They concluded that the soft flesh changed its form enough and became *tahor*, while the hard bones kept their status as human remains.)

Another example of this can be found in b.*Pesachim* 18a, where the sages discuss a hypothetical situation where an animal drinks the purification water of the red heifer. Under normal circumstances, anyone who touches this water becomes *tamei*.[21] Since an animal cannot contract impurity while it is alive, the animal does not become *tamei* when it drinks the water. But if this animal were slaughtered shortly after it drank the purification water, would the water still in its system then contaminate the animal's flesh? Rav Ashi concludes, "[The water] is completely nullified in its digestive system, since it then becomes a foul liquid." Thus, it no longer has the original properties of the purification water and it does not cause the animal's flesh to be *tamei*.

This helps us understand how food can be *tamei* when it enters a person's mouth and become *tahor* when it is expelled. The digestive process indeed purifies (makes *tahor*) all of the food that is eaten. Thus, we can understand Yeshua's statement in this way:

> Do you not see that whatever goes into a person from outside cannot compromise his holiness, since it enters not his heart but his stomach, and is expelled into the toilet, making all of the food *tahor*?

While this sentence is perfectly understandable (once you have the background information), the same grammatical problem in the Greek discussed above is present even in this English translation. Just like the grocery shopping refrigerator, the participle "making" should technically construe with "whatever goes into a person." To a grammar snob, the sentence above says that "whatever goes into a person … makes all of the food *tahor*." But a normal person will understand "making" as referring to the digestive process.

## From One Pharisee to Another

Thus, Yeshua's statement is not declarative; it is descriptive. He certainly did not make any sort of halachic ruling here. Rather, he simply used existing Jewish law as a metaphor to illustrate his ethical point.

Food that is *tamei* does not have any effect on a person's essential holiness. In fact, even when food goes in *tamei*, it comes out *tahor*. What ultimately compromises a person's essential holiness is the "impurity" generated within the person's heart: his corrupt thoughts, words, and behaviors.

The topic of *kashrut* was never raised in Yeshua's discourse, nor was the observance of ritual purity ever dismissed or condemned. Rather, he showed that the merit of care and zeal for ritual purification is completely nullified by moral degeneracy. By using Jewish law as a metaphor in this regard, he implicitly validates it.

We can now see that rather than disregarding or invalidating Torah, Yeshua upheld it. His passionate objection was in fact motivated by concern for the very heart of Torah. Thus, he is neither condemned by his own words (Matthew 5:19) or the words of Moses (Deuteronomy 13:1–5). We now find that the shock and confusion that Peter expressed when he saw the vision of the sheet (Acts 10:14) is perfectly reasonable. The concern that the apostles had regarding the food that Gentiles ate (Acts 15:20) can now be seen as in concert with their Master. And finally, Yeshua cannot be called a hypocrite for nullifying God's commandments while simultaneously accusing others of the same sin (Mark 7:9, 13).

The path of true discipleship that this passage teaches is not to expand our culinary repertoire. Rather, we learn that all of our efforts to express holiness through symbols and rituals are meaningless if there is no moral character standing behind them. Thus, we must focus on improving our thoughts, words, and deeds so that we become pure and holy internally and externally and our worship is not mere lip service. Furthermore, we must reach out to others who are perhaps not as "enlightened" as ourselves with compassion and understanding rather than ridicule and criticism. Then we will truly succeed in our efforts to be "a kingdom of priests."

## Summary: Jesus Declared All Foods Clean

When we look closely at the cultural and linguistic context of Mark 7, we find that its conventional interpretation as an abolishment of dietary law does not hold up.

- The kosher status of food is not the topic of this passage. Rather, it is about ritual purity and holiness.

- The Greek text translated "Thus he declared all foods clean" is more literally, "purifying all the foods." The words "Thus Yeshua declared" are not present in the text.

- Making foods ritually pure (*tahor*) is not the same as making foods kosher. The digestive process does in fact purify what is eaten, since dung is ritually pure.

In conclusion, we see that rather than overturning biblical or rabbinic eating standards, Yeshua simply used Jewish law to emphasize his ethical teaching about a person's essential holiness.

## Peter's Vision

Peter beheld a dramatic vision, recorded in the book of Acts.

> [Peter] saw the heavens opened and something like a great sheet descending, being let down by its four corners upon the earth. In it were all kinds of animals and reptiles and birds of the air. And there came a voice to him: "Rise, Peter; kill and eat." But Peter said, "By no means, Lord; for I have never eaten anything that is common or unclean." And the voice came to him again a second time, "What God has made clean, do not call common." This happened three times, and the thing was taken up at once to heaven. (Acts 10:11–16)

This passage is frequently cited as proof that the food laws of the Torah have come to an end. After all, God told Peter to "kill and eat" patently non-kosher animals. God has made something clean that Peter should not call common. The notes in the NIV Study Bible explain on this passage, "Jesus had already laid the groundwork for setting aside the laws of clean and unclean food." [22] The ESV Study Bible proclaims, "Verse 15 is the key: God was overturning the old clean/unclean distinctions and dietary laws in general, along with all other 'ceremonial' laws in the Mosaic covenant (including laws about sacrifices, festivals and special days, and circumcision)." [23]

## The Simple Answer

Determining the proper interpretation of Peter's vision is not difficult at all, since he explains it to us.

First, let us examine the context of the vision. Acts 10 begins by describing the experience of Cornelius, a God-fearing Gentile in Caesarea. An angel instructed him to send for Peter in Joppa.

Then we learn of Peter's dream. Its meaning was not explicit to Peter at first, which shows us that he did not assume it was meant literally. We learn that he was "inwardly perplexed as to what the vision might mean" (Acts 10:17).

In the midst of his pondering, the messengers from Cornelius arrived. The Spirit instructed him to "accompany them without hesitation" (Acts 10:20). Peter invited them in and then went with them to Caesarea the next day, entering the Gentile's home (Acts 10:25).

Finally, we see that Peter has arrived at a conclusion about the meaning of his vision, since he explained it in his own words:

> You yourselves know how unlawful it is for a Jew to associate with or to visit anyone of another nation, but God has shown me that I should not call any person common or unclean. (Acts 10:28)

He reiterated this message as he explained to them about the Messiah:

> Truly I understand that God shows no partiality, but in every nation anyone who fears him and does what is right is acceptable to him. (10:34–35)

Thus, Peter explains the message of his vision as showing that he should not treat any *person* as unclean. Peter never once interprets the vision as referring to food or any other command or prohibition.

In Acts 11, he reported his vision to his Jewish brothers[24] in Jerusalem, who had criticized them for eating with Gentiles.

> "You went to uncircumcised men and ate with them."
> (Acts 11:3)

Note that they did not accuse him of eating food that was not kosher; rather, they objected to the company that he was keeping.

(The fact that he was eating with Gentiles in a Gentile home does not require that he ate non-kosher food. It might have been that Cornelius as a pious God-fearer had been keeping many of the food laws. But even if he had not, it was fully possible for him to provide kosher food for his guest. Thus, his Jewish brothers' concern was only with the people, not the food.)

In response, Peter relates his experience and his vision. Once again, Peter's conclusion pointed to the acceptance of Gentiles:

> If then God gave the same gift to them as he gave to us when we believed in the Lord Jesus Christ, who was I that I could stand in God's way? (Acts 11:17)

The response of the brothers in Jerusalem reveals that they also understood the vision as a message of Gentile inclusion:

> When they heard these things they fell silent. And they glorified God, saying, "Then to the Gentiles also God has granted repentance that leads to life." (Acts 11:18)

The actual dietary requirements of Jews are never called into question as a response to this vision, nor do we find any examples of Jewish believers indulging in eating previously forbidden species.

## De-coding the Vision

As a prophetic parable, the animals on the sheet symbolically represent different nationalities of humans. The use of animals to symbolize nations is common in the Bible and other Jewish literature.

For example, a *midrash* (an ancient Jewish commentary) notes that the list of pure and impure animals in Leviticus mentions four specific impure animals: the camel, the hyrax (or rock badger), the hare, and the pig (Leviticus 11:4–7).[25] In this *midrash*, the Jewish sages bring proof texts to explain that these four animals allude to the four nations that would ultimately rule as empires over Israel: Babylon, Persia/Media, Greece, and Rome. They make similar connections with other animals mentioned in Scripture, including snakes, scorpions, lions, and leopards. Israel is often compared to a sheep, based on Jeremiah:

> Israel is a hunted sheep driven away by lions. First the king of Assyria devoured him, and now at last Nebuchadnezzar king of Babylon has gnawed his bones. (Jeremiah 50:17)

The sheet itself, having four corners, represents the entire earth. This alludes to Isaiah 11:12:

> He will raise a signal for the nations and will assemble the banished of Israel, and gather the dispersed of Judah from the four corners of the earth.

As we can see, the components of this vision are typical of Jewish symbolism. It is a prophetic parable. Taking this vision at face value (as if God wanted Peter to eat reptiles) without interpreting the symbolism would be like reading Daniel 7 and believing it to be about literal monstrous beasts with multiple heads and horns.

## What Law?

Peter apparently invoked Jewish law when he explained the meaning of his vision: "You yourselves know how unlawful it is for a Jew to associate with or to visit anyone of another nation" (Acts 10:28). Likewise his Jewish brothers objected (again apparently on the basis of Jewish law) that Peter "went to uncircumcised men and ate with them" (Acts 11:3).

But this is perplexing. What Jewish law forbids a Jew from associating with or entering the home of a Gentile? Even today, there is no law preventing Orthodox Jews from visiting Gentiles or eating with them.

There are some laws governing what types of food Gentiles can prepare for Jews; this is known as *bishul akum*, "what is cooked by idolaters."[26] However, there is quite a bit of leniency in these laws, which is why it is not at all uncommon to find Gentiles employed as cooks in kosher restaurants. Furthermore, the laws of *bishul akum* do not have any bearing as to *where* or *with whom* a Jewish person may eat. Thus, they do not suffice as a source of Peter's law.

In an effort to find a source, most commentators cite m.*Oholot* 18:7, which states, "The residences of Gentiles are *tamei*." However, as we learned earlier, there is no prohibition against becoming *tamei* or eating food that is *tamei*, as long as it is kosher. Ritual impurity only becomes a legal problem in the context of Temple sanctity, such as when one is eating from the offerings or entering the Temple courts. Even if a Gentile's home was built upon the gravesite of his ancestors (which was not unlikely at the time), this would not render his food non-kosher. Thus, this *mishnah* alone would not have prohibited Peter from entering the home of Cornelius or eating with him.

In Peter's vision, he reacts to the invitation to eat by saying, "By no means, Lord; for I have never eaten anything that is common or unclean" (Acts 10:14). What exactly did Peter mean by "common or unclean"? The Greek word for "common" is *koinos*, which we previously connected with the Hebrew word *chol*, the opposite of *kodesh* ("what is holy"). "Unclean" is *akathartos*, which is the equivalent of the Hebrew word *tamei* ("ritually impure").

Given that his vision included animals that are of intrinsically *tamei* species and thus not kosher, Peter might have meant, "I have never eaten anything non-kosher." However, the wording "common *or* unclean" seems to imply something beyond the baseline of kosher law. Like the Pharisees in Mark 7, Peter must have been accustomed to eating all of his meals in the condition of ritual purity. This stringency would explain why Peter would not be able to enter the homes of Gentiles.

Rabbi Yitzchak Lichtenstein interprets along these lines. He writes:

> This prohibition was conducted according to Pharisaic stringency and their rulings. They ruled that foreign lands and Gentiles were *tamei* in the time of the Second Temple, as we know from the Mishnah and Talmud, and for this reason, Romans would refer to Jews as misanthropists. Altering a Pharisaic practice is not tantamount to altering and canceling the Torah of Moses.[27]

While keeping kosher and other ceremonial aspects of Torah would not prevent the apostles from spreading Yeshua's message among Gentiles, voluntary Pharisaic abstention from all impurity would have absolutely prohibited it. Peter and the brethren in Jerusalem seem to have considered it normative if not compulsory to maintain ritual purity. Thus, God's message to Peter was not to concern himself with the impurity of the Gentiles.

## Surely Not, Lord!

The narrative of Peter's vision finds a literary antecedent in Ezekiel 4. The chapter begins with God's instructions for Ezekiel to pre-enact the siege of Jerusalem with a miniature model as a "sign for the house of Israel" (Ezekiel 4:1–3). Then he is to lie on his side for many days and "bear the iniquity" of Israel and Judah and prophesy against it (Ezekiel 4:4–8).

During the time that he lies on his side, he is to eat a certain kind of bread:

> And you, take wheat and barley, beans and lentils, millet and emmer, and put them into a single vessel and make your bread from them. (Ezekiel 4:9)

Normal, good bread is made out of fine wheat flour. But this mixture of various grains and legumes as filler symbolizes the scarcity of food under the siege and in exile. Although "Ezekiel 4:9 bread" is marketed as a health food inspired by the Bible, in context the recipe is meant to produce the worst quality bread imaginable, composed of what was normally animal fodder, in order to illustrate the suffering of the Jewish people. And thus it is to be eaten in measured rations, twenty shekels a day (about 2–3 pounds), along with only a sixth of a hin of water (about twenty-five to thirty fluid ounces).

The marketers of "Ezekiel 4:9 bread" conveniently (and thankfully) leave out the next instruction:

> "And you shall eat it as a barley cake, baking it in their sight on human dung." And the LORD said, "Thus shall the people of Israel eat their bread unclean [*tamei*], among the nations where I will drive them." (Ezekiel 4:12–13)

As noted in the discussion of Mark 7, dung is not *tamei*; it is merely "repulsive." God specifically chose dung—something repulsive but nonetheless *tahor*—to represent ritual impurity in a symbolic fashion.

Ezekiel's response to this instruction is noticeably similar to that of Peter:

> Then I said, "Ah, Lord GOD! Behold, I have never defiled myself. From my youth up till now I have never eaten what died of itself or was torn by beasts, nor has tainted meat come into my mouth." (Ezekiel 4:14)

In the Septuagint, Ezekiel's exclamation matches that of Peter exactly: *medamos kurie* (μηδαμῶς κύριε), "Surely not, Lord!"

The phrase "I have not defiled myself" is more literally, "My soul has never been made *tamei*." Jewish commentators see this as a reference to his inner purity and the purity of his thoughts. Malbim explains:

The prophet was disturbed that he was commanded to eat something repulsive that was a symbolic representation of their impurity. "My soul has never been made *tamei*" — That is to say, neither with words that contaminate the soul, nor with foods that contaminate it, nor foods that are forbidden for Jews, for "I have never eaten what died of itself or was torn by beasts," nor that which contaminates a priest (since Ezekiel was a priest), "nor has tainted meat come into my mouth," and if so, why should my mouth be aggrieved by my eating the impurity of the soul? [28]

Just as the sheet was lifted away from Peter, God relented in response to Ezekiel's objection, permitting him to use the dung of cattle instead of that of humans. This can be explained by the fact that it is less repulsive, but Malbim further interprets:

Considering your holiness and purity, cattle dung will suffice. Since it symbolically represents bodily impurity (as a cow does not have a soul), it will adequately depict what is represented by the human dung, which teaches about the impurity of the soul. Thus its message will be sufficiently clear as the desired symbol over which you will make your bread. [29]

Thus, God's message through Ezekiel was a warning that during the Babylonian exile, their food would be eaten in a state of ritual impurity. Without a Temple, there would be no way to produce food that was *tahor* (although it could still be kosher).

This is remarkable because it implies that even in the First Temple era, it was somewhat normative for common citizens to eat food in a state of ritual purity. Here we see that the ability to maintain ritual purity is a luxury of living under the shadow of the Temple. In contrast, eating food in impurity is a characteristic of exile.

Likewise, Zechariah describes the future era of redemption in terms of the ritual purity of dishes:

And every pot in Jerusalem and Judah shall be holy to the LORD of hosts, so that all who sacrifice may come and take of them and boil the meat of the sacrifice in them. (Zechariah 14:21)

We can now see the implications for Peter's vision. Peter was aware that the Temple would be destroyed and that exile was coming, since Yeshua had warned of this on multiple occasions. The "four corners of the earth" symbolized by the sheet connects with the location of the "banished of Israel" and the "dispersed of Judah" (Isaiah 11:12).

Exile is not merely a punishment; it also accomplishes a divine purpose. While scattered among the nations, the Jewish people are able to instruct and influence the nations in the way of God. This was the task that Peter and the apostles were given on the brink of the Temple's destruction.

We can now see that the similarity between Peter's vision and that of Ezekiel is not coincidental. Peter, in being shown the species representing the nations, was instructed to shed the luxury of ritual purity and embrace the mode of exile so that God's purposes could be accomplished.

### Summary: Peter's Vision

We thus learn that Peter's vision of the sheet did not serve to lift all dietary restrictions.

- Peter's vision was about people, not food. Animals represent nations in Jewish symbolism.
- No conventional law restricts Jews from eating with Gentiles. Rather, Peter was instructed to forgo a voluntary Pharisaic standard of ritual purity.
- The similarity to Ezekiel's vision highlights the connection between ritual impurity and exile.

# Answering Asceticism: Colossians 2 and 1 Timothy 4

Paul had to address many doctrinal issues in his letters to the various communities. One influence was the practice of Gnostic asceticism, a teaching that requires people to afflict themselves in order to gain supernatural revelation. This is not a practice we encounter often in the modern era. Since it is unfamiliar, people often mistake Paul's responses to these ascetic teachings for arguments against keeping kosher.

## A Shadow of Things to Come

In Colossians 2, Paul warns about a false teaching.

> Therefore let no one pass judgment on you in questions of food and drink, or with regard to a festival or a new moon or a Sabbath. These are a shadow of the things to come, but the substance belongs to Christ. (Colossians 2:16–17)

> If with Christ you died to the elemental spirits of the world, why, as if you were still alive in the world, do you submit to regulations—"Do not handle, Do not taste, Do not touch" (referring to things that all perish as they are used)—according to human precepts and teachings? (Colossians 2:20–22)

At first glance, these might seem to refute the kosher laws. But by analyzing the complete context of this passage, we will discover that this is not the case.

Paul instructs his reader not to be taken captive by "philosophy and empty deceit, according to human tradition, according to the elemental spirits of the world" (Colossians 2:8). His argument is against someone "insisting on asceticism and worship of angels, going on in detail about visions, puffed up without reason by his sensuous mind" (Colossians 2:18). These regulations are "according to human precepts and teachings" (Colossians 2:22) and promote "self-made religion and asceticism and severity to the body" (Colossians 2:23).

These descriptions have nothing to do with kosher law or the Torah. As the text explicitly states, Paul is addressing asceticism.

## The Fullness of Deity

Paul begins his refutation by explaining that in the Messiah "the whole fullness of deity dwells bodily, and you have been filled in him" (Colossians 2:9–10). In other words, God's Spirit dwells in us by virtue of Yeshua.

Talmudic sages also use the indwelling Spirit to refute the idea of self affliction. In the context of fasting, they cite the opinion of Rabbi Eli'ezer:

> A person should always regard himself as if the Holy One resides within his body, as it is said, "… the Holy One in your midst, and I will not come in wrath"[30] (Hosea 11:9). (b. *Ta'anit* 11a–b)

Rashi explains this as meaning that a person should regard himself "as if all of his body is holy, and it is forbidden to weaken it."[31] Weakening one's body makes it more difficult to carry out important commandments and good deeds. It also is not befitting the honor of the divine presence within the person.

## Canceling the Record of Debt

Next, Paul addresses the idea that one must flagellate himself due to his corrupt and mortal condition. He refutes this by speaking of the renewal that accompanies faith:

> In him also you were circumcised with a circumcision made without hands, by putting off the body of the flesh, by the circumcision of Christ, having been buried with him in baptism, in which you were also raised with him through faith in the powerful working of God, who raised him from the dead. (Colossians 2:11–12)

This is a reference to Deuteronomy, which promises:

> And the LORD your God will circumcise your heart and the heart of your offspring, so that you will love the LORD your God with all your heart and with all your soul, that you may live. (Deuteronomy 30:6)

The circumcision of the heart is not accompanied by abrogation of the Torah, but by renewed observance:

And you shall again obey the voice of the LORD and keep all his commandments that I command you today. (Deuteronomy 30:8)

Paul continues by showing that one need not punish himself on account of his past sins, because through repentance and faith in Yeshua, we receive forgiveness of sins:

And you, who were dead in your trespasses and the uncircumcision of your flesh, God made alive together with him, having forgiven us all our trespasses, by canceling the record of debt that stood against us with its legal demands. This he set aside, nailing it to the cross. He disarmed the rulers and authorities and put them to open shame, by triumphing over them in him. (Colossians 2:13–15)

The reference to the "record of debt" coincides with Jewish belief about sin, punishment, and repentance:

Rabbi Yitzchak says: Four things tear up the decree of a man's sentence: charity, crying out [in prayer], changing one's name, and changing one's behavior. (b.*Rosh HaShanah* 16b)

The "rulers and authorities" represent spiritual powers that prosecute or accuse the individual, seeking divine retribution. They are utterly refuted and can no longer make any claim against the person.

## Let No One Pass Judgment

Paul effectively refutes the argument of the ascetics by pointing to the indwelling Spirit, the regeneration that accompanies faith, and the forgiveness of sins. He continues by affirming the proper behavior of his readers:

Therefore let no one pass judgment on you in questions of food and drink, or with regard to a festival or a new moon or a Sabbath. These are a shadow of the things to come, but the substance belongs to Christ. (Colossians 2:16–17)

That is to say, let none of these preachers of asceticism criticize you for enjoying food or partaking of wine. They should not pass judgment on you for participating in celebration, relaxation, and mild indulgence on the holidays, new-moon celebrations, or the Sabbath day. These observances are a "shadow of things to come" (Colossians 2:17).

Judaism teaches that the enjoyment of the holidays is a fore-taste of the utopian messianic future. The Talmud explains that the Sabbath is "one-sixtieth part[32] of the age to come."[33] The popular Sabbath table hymn *Mah Yedidut* declares,

> A semblance of the World to Come
>   is the Sabbath Day of contentment,
> All who delight in it
>   will merit much gladness[34]

Paul does not mean to say that we have already entered the messianic future. Rather, this future time will come with the glorious return of the Messiah, when the world will be characterized by peace, blessing, and abundance. Nonetheless, by saying that "the substance belongs to Christ" (Colossians 2:17), Paul teaches that the Messiah is not merely a hint or foretaste of the age to come—he is an actual part of it. The Messiah has entered "beyond the veil," so to speak, and as his followers, we are able in some sense to experience the realized messianic hope even today. How much more so, then, should we be permitted enjoyment in this life!

Therefore, we see that when Paul's opponents insist "Do not handle, Do not taste, Do not touch" (Colossians 2:21), they are not speaking of the God-given commandments but "human precepts" (Colossians 2:22). These are the laws of "self-made religion and asceticism and severity to the body" (Colossians 2:23). In contrast, the Torah teaches that we may "eat and be satisfied" with the foods permitted to us, provided that we "bless the LORD" (Deuteronomy 8:10). The delight we experience in this life is only a small hint of what is in store for those who are faithful to him.

### Summary: A Shadow of Things to Come

Colossians 2 cannot be used to overturn kosher law. The topic of the passage is about the man-made heresy of Gnostic asceticism, not the biblical practice of eating kosher. Paul refutes the ascetic heresy by explaining:

- It is inappropriate to afflict oneself needlessly, because of God's indwelling Spirit.
- One need not afflict himself due to his corrupt, mortal condition, because a person's condition is renewed by faith.
- One need not punish himself for past sins, because a person's sins are forgiven through repentance.
- One is permitted to experience enjoyment on the Sabbath and holidays, because they are a foretaste of the messianic age to come.

## Nothing Is to Be Rejected

Paul's words in 1 Timothy 4:1–5 provide another source of objection to the Bible's kosher laws.

> Now the Spirit expressly says that in later times some will depart from the faith by devoting themselves to deceitful spirits and teachings of demons, through the insincerity of liars whose consciences are seared, who forbid marriage and require abstinence from foods that God created to be received with thanksgiving by those who believe and know the truth. For everything created by God is good, and nothing is to be rejected if it is received with thanksgiving, for it is made holy by the word of God and prayer.

But the people who "depart from the faith" do not advocate a Torah-observant lifestyle. According to the interpretation of Jewish law, marriage is an ideal state of existence:

> Rabbi Tanchum cited Rabbi Chanilai, saying: Any man who has no wife lives without joy, without blessing, and without goodness. Without joy, as it is said, "You shall rejoice—you and your household [interpreted as a euphemism for 'wife']" (Deuteronomy 14:26). Without blessing, as it is said, "That a blessing may rest on your household" (Ezekiel 44:30). Without goodness, as it is

said, "It is not good for man to be alone" (Genesis 2:18).
(b.*Yevamot* 62b)[35]

Having children is considered an obligation (under normal circumstances) to fulfill the commandment, "Be fruitful and multiply" (Genesis 1:28).[36]

The objects of Paul's condemnation are those who teach against both marriage and eating certain foods. His opponent must be someone other than a person wanting to keep kosher.

## The Teaching of Demons

Paul has a very high level of respect for the Torah. He would never refer to it as the "teachings of demons" (1 Timothy 4:1) or "irreverent, silly myths" (1 Timothy 4:7). Instead he calls the Torah and commandments "holy, righteous, and good" (Romans 7:12) and "the oracles of God" (Romans 3:2).

Paul instructed Timothy to devote himself "to the public reading of Scripture, to exhortation, to teaching" (1 Timothy 4:13). But the New Testament had not been fully written, much less canonized at the time. To Paul and Timothy, "Scripture" meant the Old Testament. When he speaks against this teaching, he cannot be referring to the God-given dietary laws.

## Everything is Good

Paul's argument against his opponents is based on the premise that "everything created by God is good" (1 Timothy 4:4). If Paul's point were that because of this there are no limits whatsoever as to what people can eat, it would not be a sound argument. First of all, the mere fact that God instituted the food laws after having created everything would refute it. Second, God also created poisonous and unhealthy substances which cannot be consumed even though they are presumably "good." Third, even a person who did not advocate kosher laws would uphold some limits, such as cannibalism, stolen food, drunkenness, or overeating.[37]

But what is the solution? Paul's words should be contextualized just like those of any other Jewish sage. For example, the Jerusalem Talmud records:

Rabbi Hezekiah and Rabbi Kohen cited Rav: "In the future, a person will need to give justification and an accounting for all that his eye saw but he did not eat." (y.*Kiddushin* 4:12)

If Paul had said this, people would assume that he taught the abrogation of the Torah's food laws. But no one would imagine these Talmudic sages as teaching this. They are merely teaching against asceticism—the belief that abstaining from physical pleasure is a pious act. Abraham Cohen explains:

> A characteristic attitude is taken up by the Talmud towards the pleasures of life. Recognizing that what has been created by God for man's enjoyment must be essentially good, it not only counsels men to indulge in them but even condemns those who abstain from them. The Rabbis assume the standpoint that God wants His creatures to be happy, and it must therefore be sinful deliberately to shun physical happiness and material well-being.[38]

The Didache, a Christian document from the early second century, presents a similar statement in the context of its after-meal blessing:

> You, almighty Master, created all things for your name's sake; you gave food and drink for human beings to enjoy so that they would give thanks to you. (Didache 10:3)

This suggests that Paul's opponents are ascetics who believed that sanctification could only occur through abstaining from pleasure. Paul's response is that enjoyment is sanctified through the word of God and prayer.

Food is sanctified by the word of God in that by honoring the parameters that God has established for food, eating becomes an act of worship and sanctity. The Torah explains the kosher laws as a matter of holiness:

> You shall not eat anything that has died naturally. You may give it to the sojourner who is within your towns, that he

may eat it, or you may sell it to a foreigner. For you are a people holy to the LORD your God. (Deuteronomy 14:21)

For I am the LORD your God. Consecrate yourselves therefore, and be holy, for I am holy. You shall not defile yourselves with any swarming thing that crawls on the ground. (Leviticus 11:44)

Likewise, food is sanctified by prayer in that eating and enjoying food becomes an opportunity to recite blessings of thanks.

Our Rabbis have taught: It is forbidden for a person to derive enjoyment from the world without saying a blessing. Whoever derives enjoyment from the world without saying a blessing has committed the sin of desecration.[39] (b.*Brachot* 35a)

In contrast, animals have no means to sanctify food. They have no discretion as to what they eat, nor are they able to express thanks to God for providing it. They eat only to satisfy their urges rather than to enable themselves to serve their Creator.

The same can be said for sex. Sex is inherently good, but it is not inherently sacred. It only becomes sanctified when it is enjoyed within the proper parameters that God established in his Word.

## Summary: Nothing Is to Be Rejected

Paul's letter to Timothy did not instruct him to stop keeping kosher. We can see this because:

- Paul's opponents are not Torah-keepers. Their abstinence from food should not be assumed to be kosher observance.
- Paul characterizes their teachings in derogatory terms. He would never speak this way about the Torah.
- Paul's assertion that "everything is good" must be understood in context. It simply shows that we need not abstain from pleasure.

- The word of God sanctifies food by providing parameters around what may be eaten. Prayer sanctifies food by making eating an act of worship.

As we can see, argumentation against asceticism does not amount to refuting kosher laws. Rather, we learn that we should not abstain from things simply on the basis of avoiding pleasure. Instead, we should enjoy what God has permitted to us and use the opportunity to offer blessings of thanks.

## The Weak in Faith: Romans 14

In Romans 14, Paul seems to lay down the line regarding kosher food. While Mark 7 and Acts 10 are matters of ritual purity, this is not a plausible explanation for Romans, since Rome is outside of the land of Israel and maintaining true ritual purity would be impossible.[40] Furthermore, it is clear in this passage that it is the food itself that is the problematic issue rather than people or places.

Paul speaks of those who are "weak in faith." These are typically understood to represent Jewish Christians who mistakenly maintain Jewish observances because their faith in their freedom in Christ is deficient. However, there is no explicit indication of this. All we know about the "weak" from this passage is that they abstain from eating meat.

Kosher law does not require anyone to abstain from all meat. Thus, it cannot be assumed that those who abstain do so simply for kosher reasons. But why else would someone abstain from meat?

Another question arises from Paul's instructions for the "strong." While he categorizes himself along with the "strong," he does not criticize or correct the "weak" at all. Rather, he warns the "strong" not to cast judgment on their opinions, but to accommodate their weakness. It seems as though he places both positions on equal footing, since both groups are acting out of a desire to serve God. (Most commentators on this passage fall into the trap of casting judgment on the "weaker brother" in this passage, which is exactly what Paul says not to do. This inconsistency is what Nanos refers to as "Luther's trap."[41]) Why would Paul identify as "strong," but then affirm the "weak" stance and admonish only the "strong"?

Finally, while Romans 14 focuses on eating food, a brief reference is made to the observance of days. Traditionally, this is understood to refer to the weekly Sabbath or Jewish holidays, although the text does not state this. What is the reason for bringing days into the discussion and how do they relate to eating food?

## I Will Never Eat Meat

Paul uses similar terminology in his letter to the Corinthians. Paul responded to the Corinthian assertion that "as to the eating of food offered to idols, we know that 'an idol has no real existence,'" by explaining, "However, not all possess this knowledge. But some, through former association with idols, eat food as really offered to an idol, and their conscience, being *weak*, is defiled." Although the Corinthians maintain, "Food will not commend us to God. We are no worse off if we do not eat, and no better off if we do," Paul responds,

> But take care that this right of yours does not somehow become a stumbling block to the *weak*. For if anyone sees you who have knowledge eating in an idol's temple, will he not be encouraged, if his conscience is *weak*, to eat food offered to idols? And so by your knowledge this *weak* person is destroyed, the brother for whom Christ died. Thus, sinning against your brothers and wounding their conscience when it is *weak*, you sin against Christ. Therefore, if food makes my brother stumble, *I will never eat meat*, lest I make my brother stumble.

From this we see that Paul uses the term "weak" to describe people who were formerly associated with idol worship—individuals who are far more likely to be Gentiles than Jews. The reason that they abstain from meat is due to concern that it may be associated with idol worship, not because of kosher laws such as the species of animal, its method of slaughter, or its combination with dairy. Perhaps the ties to idolatry bring up painful memories of their past. Alternatively, the exposure to idolatry may entice the former pagan to backslide and indulge once again in paganism. Either way, Paul makes it clear that the risk involved is not worth it; like the apostles ruled in Acts 15, meat offered to idols must be avoided, if only to avoid harming the "weak."

This helps explain why in Romans 14, Paul does not attempt to correct or criticize the "weak" as being in error. Instead, he admonishes the "strong" to concede to the sensitivity of the "weak" without casting judgment. At the same time, Paul categorizes himself along with the "strong." This does not necessarily mean that he is comfortable eating meat offered to idols; it simply refers to the fact that he does not come from an idolatrous background and thus is not sensitive to pagan influences.

Alcoholism is a fitting analogy. The Bible does not prohibit the consumption of alcohol in moderation. Nonetheless, for a person who is recovering from alcoholism or who has suffered from someone else's alcohol abuse, the mere presence of sacramental wine at a Sabbath table may be destructive. As much as one might enjoy his Sabbath wine, it would be wrong to make it a stumbling block for his brother. Paul says, "We who are strong have an obligation to bear with the [weaknesses[42]] of the weak, and not to please ourselves" (Romans 15:1).

However, this case is different because the "weak" see their prohibition as legally binding, not just a matter of comfort. They are in good company, too, since the apostles specifically ruled that Gentiles should stay away from things that are offered to idols (Acts 15:20, 29; 21:25).

Paul's attitude is reflected in the Gemara:

> How do we know that one should not extend a cup of wine to a Nazarite[43] or the limb from a live animal to a *Ben Noach*?[44] It is taught by the verse, "You should not place an obstacle before the blind" (Leviticus 19:14). (b.*Avodah Zarah* 6b)

> Things that are permitted, yet others are accustomed to treat them as forbidden, you are not allowed to permit in their presence. (b.*Pesachim* 50b–51a, b.*Megillah* 5b, b.*Nedarim* 15a, 81b)

## Cooked By Idolaters?

It is possible that the food in question is not actually offered to idols *per se*. Rather, it may merely be included in the halachic category of things contaminated by idolatry simply by virtue of originating from Gentiles. Rabbinic safeguards prohibit certain foods including meat, wine, and cheese if they are produced by Gentiles. Some of these concerns have to do with possible contamination by non-kosher ingredients, but many also have to do with idolatry.

An early form of the prohibition of *bishul akum*, "what is cooked by idolaters," (and related prohibitions) could be in play here. From the halachic perspective of these laws, a Gentile falls in the category of *akum* ("idolators," literally, "worshipers of stars and constellations") even if he is a God-fearer who has rejected idolatry. Perhaps the "weak" are those who feel compelled to maintain strict observance of these laws, whereas the strong feel confident enough to exclude Gentile followers of Yeshua from the ban.

Tomson proposes a similar idea:

> Thus it seems that the food problem in Rom 14 was complex. At one level Paul's plea appears to have been for willingness on the part of gentile Christians to make allowances for basic Jewish food laws. On another level, he argued that gentile Christians should also bear with 'hyper-halakhic' anxieties regarding gentile wine and meat. As we have seen the details are not quite decisive and we have to leave both possibilities open.[45]

Nonetheless, Tomson admits that this implies that Paul was two-sided, on the one hand railing against Peter at Antioch, and yet instructing others to bear with the "weak" without criticizing them:

> Nevertheless this conclusion is astonishing. It means that in Romans and Galatians Paul argued diametrically opposed cases: at Antioch he would have openly withstood 'hyper-sensitive' Jews who made trouble for the gentiles, while in Rom 14 he appeals to gentiles to be tolerant towards such over-sensitive Jews![46]

At any rate, whether the food was actually idol-contaminated or merely incriminated by association with Gentiles, we can see that idolatry—not *kashrut*—was the primary issue.

## Being Mindful of Days

The text makes a brief digression into discussing calendar observances:

> One person esteems one day as better than another, while another esteems all days alike. Each one should be fully convinced in his own mind. The one who observes the day, observes it in honor of the Lord. The one who eats, eats in honor of the Lord, since he gives thanks to God, while the one who abstains, abstains in honor of the Lord and gives thanks to God. (Romans 14:5–6)

There are issues with both the translation and the interpretation of this passage. As for the translation, the problems are numerous:

- **"Esteems"** : The Greek word translated "esteems" is *krino* (κρίνω). This simply means "to judge." Throughout the book of Romans, Paul uses the term to mean "to pass judgment," i.e., "to condemn." For example, this is the term that Paul uses in verse 3 of this chapter to say, "Let not the one who abstains *pass judgment* on the one who eats." It can also be used to mean "to make a determination" (e.g., Acts 15:19). Lexicons that list "prefer" or "esteem highly" among the meanings do so primarily on the basis of its use in Romans 14, thus making it circular reasoning. Thus, our passage should read, "One person *judges* one day … while another *judges* all days alike."
- **"As better than"** : The phrase "as better than" does not appear in Greek. Rather, there is only the simple and versatile preposition *para* (παρά). With an accusative noun, *para* is used to draw a comparison or contrast, but it does not have any intrinsically positive value. Thus, a more accurate translation would be "One person judges one day

*in contrast with* another, while another judges all days alike."

- **"Observes"** : The Greek term translated "observes" is *froneo* (φρονέω). It means "to think, to be mindful of, or to hold an opinion." It does not mean "observe" in the sense of celebrating or commemorating a holiday or practicing a commandment. For example, in Romans 8:5 Paul uses the term in the statement, "Those who live according to the flesh *set their minds on* the things of the flesh." Thus, our passage would be better translated, "The one who *is mindful of* a day *is mindful of it* ..."

- **"In honor of"** : No Greek word for "honor" appears here. The word for "Lord" (*kurios*, κύριος) is merely in the dative case (*kurio*, κυρίῳ). So while it is "to the Lord" in some sense, it does not necessarily imply what "in honor of" implies.

Ultimately, a more objective translation of this passage reads:

> One person judges one day in contrast with another, while another judges all days alike. Each one should be fully convinced in his own mind. The one who is mindful of the day is mindful of it for the Lord. The one who eats, eats for the Lord, since he gives thanks to God, while the one who abstains, abstains for the Lord and gives thanks to God.

It should be noted that certain things are *not* stated in this passage. First, there is no indication that these are days of the week, of the month, of the year, or if they are one-time events. Second, there is no mention as to whether these days are major Jewish holy days, minor Jewish fasts or observances, civil events, or pagan holidays. Third, as our translation shows, there is no indication that either the "strong" or the "weak" looks at these days in a positive way at all, only that some are "mindful" of them, whereas others are apparently not.

Paul inserts this mention of days into a larger discussion about food and through parallelism draws a comparison between the days and the food. This means that our explanation for the days has to correlate to the explanation for food. Given that the topic at hand is the question of eating food offered to idols and that the "weak" represent people with former association with idolatry, it makes sense that the "days" at hand also relate to idol worship. This is not to say that anyone condoned celebrating a pagan holiday, but in a community saturated with foreign religion, their holidays and observances would loom over the believers. Should one modify their behavior on these idolatrous days so as to avoid association with them (i.e., be mindful of the day), or would it be better to ignore their existence altogether (i.e., treat every day alike)?

For example, tractate *Avodah Zarah* in the Mishnah opens with a discussion of activities that were prohibited during Roman holidays.[47] These holidays were avoided so as to prevent the idolaters from rejoicing and giving thanks to their deities:

> Three days prior to festivals of the Gentiles, it is prohibited to engage in business with them, to lend anything to them, or to borrow from them, to lend them money or to borrow money from them, to repay them or to accept payment from them. Rabbi Judah says: We should accept payment from him because it causes him distress. They said to him: Even though it causes him distress at first, later he will be happy [to be out of debt].

> Rabbi Ishmael says: It is prohibited three days prior and three days afterward. The sages say: Prior to their festival it is prohibited, but afterward it is permitted.

> These are the festivals of the Gentiles: Kalenda, Saturnalia, Kratesis, the inauguration day of kings, [the king's] birthday, and the anniversary of [the king's] death (according to Rabbi Meir). The sages say: On any death where they held a burning, it is considered idolatry. If they did not hold a burning, it is not idolatry. On the occasion of [a Gentile's] haircut or shaving his beard, on the day when one completed a sea voyage, on a day when one was released from prison, or if a Gentile made a banquet for his son, it is only prohibited on that day and with that particular individual. (m.*Avodah Zarah* 1:1–3)

The concern about food thus parallels the concern about certain days, and fits neatly into Paul's discussion:

|  | Meat and Wine | Days |
|---|---|---|
| *Weak position* | One should abstain from meat or wine offered to idols, so as to avoid the appearance of worshiping the idol. | One should modify one's behavior during pagan observances, so as to avoid the appearance of observing the day. |
| *Strong position* | One should ignore the idolatrous provenance of the meat or wine, since obsessing over it implicitly acknowledges the reality of false gods. | One should ignore the idolatrous significance of the day, since obsessing over it implicitly acknowledges that it has some true meaning. |

## Nothing is Unclean

The point of Paul's letter is not to declare which position is right. Rather, he wanted his readers to understand that both parties ought to respect one another's opinions since both are motivated by an effort to please God.

As he concludes the discussion of this topic, Paul asserts:

> I know and am persuaded in the Lord Jesus that nothing is unclean [*koinos*] in itself, but it is unclean for anyone who thinks it unclean. (Romans 14:14)

This statement must be taken in context and cannot be construed in absolute terms. After all, Revelation says that in the New Jerusalem,

> ... nothing unclean [*koinos*] will ever enter it, nor anyone who does what is detestable or false, but only those who are written in the Lamb's book of life. (Revelation 21:27)

But in this chapter, the topic at hand is the permissibility of meat and wine offered to idols—not all things or even all foods. By saying that nothing is *koinos* in itself, he does not mean that nothing is *koinos* period, as if "uncleanness" is imaginary. Rather, he simply acknowledges that it is legally defined, and rightly so. Some communities will hold to a position that prohibits a specific item, and others will hold to a position that permits it. Both positions are arrived at through careful study and application of the Scriptures. Since God affirms the halachic process of both, they should mutually respect one another's opinions.

The idea that ritual purity is not intrinsic is reflected in the midrashic text, *Pesikta DeRav Kahana*:

> A certain Gentile objected to Rabbi Yochanan ben Zakkai: "The things that you do seem to be a type of magic. You bring a cow and slaughter it and burn it, and pound it, and take its ashes. Then when one of you becomes *tamei* from a corpse, you sprinkle it on them two or three times and say to him 'You are *tahor*.'"[48]

Yochanan ben Zakkai meets his objection by explaining that it is not much different from the Gentiles' own exorcism practices. But his disciples seek a better answer:

> "By your lives, a corpse does not actually contaminate, nor does water actually purify. Rather, it is simply a ruling of the King of kings of kings. The blessed Holy One said, 'I have made a decree; I have made a ruling. No man has the authority to transgress my ruling, as it says, "This is the decree of the Torah" (Numbers 19:2).'"[49]

Thus, Yochanan ben Zakkai upholds that ritual purity is a legal matter rather than something natural or intrinsic.

### Summary: The Weak in Faith in Romans 14

As we can see, while Romans 14 is about food, it is not about *kashrut* in general but about the question of meat and wine offered to idols.

- The "weak" are not Torah-observant Jews as commonly supposed, but Gentiles who were involved in idolatry during their former lives.

- Paul is "strong" in that he has no sensitivity to idolatry, but he supports the right of the "weak" to hold their halachic position against idol meat.

The main message of Romans 14 is that brothers should seek peace and mutual understanding and accommodate the needs of others, even if they do not understand or agree with their positions.

# PART 2

# WHAT THE TORAH SAYS ABOUT KASHRUT

Kosher is the Hebrew word for "fit" or "proper."[50] Its most frequent use today is in regard to foods that meet the requirements of the Jewish dietary laws. The kosher laws in Judaism begin with the instructions in the Bible about what we may or may not eat, upon which Jewish scholars and teachers have expounded and expanded.

## Introduction

A majority of the kosher laws pertain to meat and other animal products, although there are many issues that concern plants as well. Some aspects of keeping kosher are simple and up-front, such as animals that cannot be eaten. Others are far more subtle and require a close look at what the Torah says. Some things are made more complicated in our modern age where food processing is much different from that of Bible times.

Some of the kosher laws are easier to understand if one is familiar with ancient agricultural practices. Some of the laws must also be seen in the light of the ritual purity laws of the ancient Tabernacle, its sacrifices, and the priesthood. In certain cases, a firm grasp of the Hebrew language is necessary to prevent misunderstandings.

## Pure and Impure Animals

A clear starting point for biblical dietary laws is the list of pure and impure animals. This list is given in two places in the Torah: Leviticus chapter 11 and Deuteronomy chapter 14.

Although the Torah uses the term *tahor* ("pure") and *tamei* ("impure") to describe permitted and prohibited species of animals, these terms might be misleading.

First of all, animals are not actually *tamei* unless they are dead. Thus, an on-duty priest would not be prohibited from touching a live donkey, camel, or dog. Animals that are of an intrinsically *tamei* species become *tamei* when they die. Animals that are of an intrinsically *tahor* species could possibly remain *tahor* if they are properly slaughtered, although they become *tamei* if they die under other circumstances.

Second, as discussed earlier, food does not have to be *tahor* to be kosher. "Pure" and "kosher" are not synonyms. However, the Torah instructs both that these species are intrinsically *tamei* and that they are not to be eaten.

The Torah groups animals into the following categories:

- large, four-footed land animals
- water animals
- flying animals
- teeming creatures that fly or crawl

The Bible classifies animals in a different manner from modern biology. For example, whales fit into the same category as fish, while bats fit together with birds. Biblical taxonomy seems to place more focus on the domain in which the creature lives, rather than its physical characteristics.

With most classifications, the Torah lists physical traits that identify intrinsically pure animals, as well as offering examples of some that are pure and impure. With birds, the Torah does not indicate any physical characteristics, but only presents a list.

## Large Land Animals (Leviticus 11:1–8; Deuteronomy 14:4–9)

The Hebrew term *behemah* (בְּהֵמָה) refers to any of various large land animals, typically mammals. Large land animals are permitted if they meet two criteria:

- The animal must have split hooves.

- The animal must chew (literally, "bring up") the cud. This means that the animal ruminates, regurgitating semi-digested food in order to chew it again.

Leviticus 11 and Deuteronomy 14 offer these examples of disqualified animals: camel, rock badger, hare, and pig. Deuteronomy 14 also offers these examples of pure animals: ox, sheep, goat, deer, gazelle, roebuck, wild goat, ibex, antelope, and mountain sheep.

The requirement of split hooves is actually a double requirement:

- it must have hooves, as opposed to toes or paws, for example, and
- the hooves must be split in the middle, rather than being one solid piece

Following the prescribed pattern, we could safely identify several other pure species. For example: bison, elk, giraffe, yak, and water buffalo all meet the requirements. Dogs, horses, kangaroos, and llamas do not.

We would do well not to take this simple kosher law for granted, since it can have complex implications. Most of the time, when eating red meat, it is easy to tell that it came from a kosher species. There is not normally any reasonable concern that if you order a steak at a restaurant you may unknowingly receive a pork chop instead. However, pork products appear in many prepared foods, even those that do not appear to contain meat. In some cuisines, lard (pork fat) is often used in place of butter and is a common ingredient in pastries and pie crusts. It is experiencing resurgence in popularity due to the health warnings concerning trans-fat oils.[51] Bacon and pork stock are sometimes used as a flavoring. Pig skin and bones are major sources of gelatin,[52] which can be found in an incredible range of foods. "All beef" sausages may have pork casings.[53] And believe it or not, ground beef from the supermarket may very well have small but significant amounts of other meats:

> Dateline NBC conducted an investigation in 1998 to determine if what was being sold as pure ground beef was really that. They submitted 100 samples from different

stores to an USDA recognized lab with 29 of those samples testing positive for meats other than ground beef. Even health food stores like Fresh Fields and Wild Oats sold adulterated ground beef.[54]

Restaurants are notorious in this regard, and this issue is compounded by the fact that ingredient lists are not always easily available. Vegetable soup often has a meat broth. In many restaurant recipes, ham and bacon are secret ingredients that give dishes a savory zest. Think the bean burritos are safe? Mexican staple dishes such as refried beans or tortillas are quite often cooked with lard. All of these factors are significant and must be considered if one is to keep a biblical standard of kosher.

### Water Animals (Leviticus 11:9–12; Deuteronomy 14:9–10)

Water animals are simply referred to in Scripture as "all that is in the water," or *kol asher bamayim* (כֹּל אֲשֶׁר בַּמָּיִם).

Aquatic life, no matter how it is classified biologically, is subject to two conditions in order to be kosher:

- The animal must have fins.
- The animal must have scales.

Historically, this has been taken to refer to the typical type of fins and scales you find on most fish. All crustaceans and cephalopods are impure, as well as smooth-skinned sharks, eels, and catfish. Common kosher fish include salmon, tilapia, trout, tuna, walleye, bass, cod, and mahi-mahi.

There is some uncertainty about what actually qualifies as a scale. Sturgeons, for example, have scale-like bony plates on their skin, but they are different from those of other fish. In cases like this, we need more information about what is meant by a "scale" (Hebrew: *kaskeset*, קַשְׂקֶשֶׂת) in order to determine whether or not the fish is kosher.

It is important to remember that the biblical understanding of a word or concept may not match the scientific definition of its English translation. Thus, it is pointless to look at English dictionaries or biology textbooks to determine what is or is not a "scale" as it pertains to biblical kosher law. According to a strictly scientific standard, even sharks and rays have scales.[55]

It is sometimes helpful to look at a word's etymology (linguistic historical origin) to determine its meaning, but that can also be misleading, as the meanings of words change over time and sometimes have little or nothing to do with their etymological roots.[56] It is occasionally helpful to compare the words with related terms in other languages, but this can also lead one astray, since words can drastically change meaning as they go from one people group to another.[57] The safest way to define a word is to consider how the culture has defined the term historically.

Jewish law has come to a specific definition of a scale. If it can be removed from the animal's skin without causing significant damage, then it qualifies as a scale as it pertains to kosher law.[58] By this definition, a sturgeon would not be kosher.

People often note that impure fish frequently tend to be "bottom feeders." However, it is important to note that the text does not base a marine animal's kosher status on where or what it eats. A fish may very well be a bottom feeder, yet perfectly meet the requirements for kosher status. Carp is one example of such a fish.

Just as in the case of pork, non-kosher marine animals frequently find their way into processed foods. Vegetable stir-fry at an Asian restaurant may very well have a non-kosher fish sauce. One cannot assume that fish sandwiches are necessarily a kosher species. For example, McDonald's famous Filet-O-Fish includes hoki (also known as blue grenadier or blue hake), which is not kosher.[59]

Once a fish has been skinned and filleted, the species cannot be positively identified. Many non-kosher fish fillets look identical to kosher fillets, so it is entirely possible that a fish may be misidentified or mislabeled at a store. *Kashrut* agencies often recommend purchasing fillets that still have at least a small amount of skin, so that even if it is misidentified, it will still be clear that the fish is from a kosher species.

This recommendation has proven to be exceedingly prudent. In their December issue, Consumer Reports Magazine published the results of an investigation into fish fraud. They sent samples of fresh and frozen fish to a lab for DNA testing to see if the species of fish matched the label.

More than one-fifth of 190 pieces of seafood we bought at retail stores and restaurants in New York, New Jersey, and Connecticut were mislabeled as different species of fish, incompletely labeled, or misidentified by employees.[60]

The Boston Globe conducted a similar investigation and reported that

Overall, the testing revealed that nearly half of 183 fish samples collected at restaurants and supermarkets were not the species ordered.[61]

The Globe's report included a story about how executives from the T. G. I. Friday's restaurant chain became suspicious when the "Key West grouper" they had purchased from a supplier had an unusual color and texture. Upon further investigation it turned out that the fish they received and served in over 500 restaurants was the far less expensive and lower quality Vietnamese catfish.[62]

Fish are often called by several common names, which may also lead to mistaken identity. For example, although true salmon is kosher, "rock salmon" is a common term for the flesh of the spiny dogfish, a non-kosher fish often used in fish-and-chips shops in the United Kingdom.[63]

## Birds (Leviticus 11:13–19; Deuteronomy 14:11–18)

"Birds" is a case in point in regards to biblical definitions. While modern biology does not include bats among the taxonomic class of birds, the Bible groups them together into one category. The term in Hebrew used here for a bird (ohf, עוֹף) comes from a verbal root meaning "to fly," although some of the species of birds listed cannot actually fly.[64]

In each of the other categories of animals, the Bible gives us general rules by which we can determine whether or not a species of animal is kosher. With birds, no such rule is given. People often look at the list of species prohibited by the Bible and note that many of them appear to be birds of prey or scavengers; however, it is critical to note that Scripture never mentions such a pattern. Rather, the text seems to indicate that there is a considerable but finite list of non-kosher birds. It would appear that all other birds may be eaten, regardless of their physical characteristics or diet.

However, we are presented with a serious problem regarding the list of non-kosher birds. Jewish tradition is uncertain about the exact identity of many of the twenty birds that are proscribed. Most of the time we take for granted the important role Jewish tradition plays in preserving the meanings of Hebrew words. If it had not been for Jewish tradition, Hebrew would be as obscure as the language of the ancient Mayans. It is only because of Jewish tradition that we can read and translate the Hebrew Bible. The meanings of many words (such as *tzitzit*, צִיצִת) would be a complete mystery. The vocalization of the text (i.e., the placement of vowels and accents), which can have a significant impact on meaning, could only be speculated since it was preserved orally until about one millennium ago. For that matter, it was Jewish tradition that decided what books are authoritative and included in the canon in the first place. But in this case, we are at a loss because tradition is unable to provide us with answers.

Our English translations, unfortunately, do not typically communicate that uncertainty. They do their best to find a likely candidate for each bird named and leave it at that. This is particularly the case in Christian translations, where the editors would see no practical reason for someone to need to know the exact identity of each bird, since they believe that kosher law no longer applies.[65] Among Jewish Bibles, the JPS Tanakh (Jewish Publication Society) mentions in a footnote that "a number of these cannot be identified with certainty," and the Stone Edition Tanach (ArtScroll/Mesorah Publications) leaves many of them untranslated with suggestions in footnotes.

As a result of that uncertainty, the Jewish community has taken the approach that to be safe, one must only eat birds for which there is a reliable tradition that it is kosher. This may seem like a drastic measure, but it is the only way to be certain to avoid the species that are off-limits.

Some of the birds that are considered "safe" are chicken, ducks, geese, turkeys,[66] pheasants, doves, and pigeons. Most birds typically eaten in Western cultures fall into this category, although recently ostrich and emu (both non-kosher) farms have become more mainstream.[67]

*Teeming Creatures (Leviticus 11:20–23,*
*29–31, 41–45; Deuteronomy 14:19–20)*

The Torah speaks of another distinct class of animals known as "teeming creatures" (*sheretz*, שֶׁרֶץ). This term is translated differently depending on the circumstances but generally refers to small, crawling animals. In some cases, it is translated as "insects," but it is important to note that it is irrelevant whether or not the animal meets the scientific definition of an insect. The term *sheretz* includes bugs of all kinds, worms, rodents, amphibians, and reptiles. Any kind of creepy-crawly creature can be called a *sheretz*. An all-inclusive translation of the term might be "vermin."

The Torah divides this group into two categories: those that fly and those on the ground. (In other contexts, the term is used of creatures in the water as well,[68] but in this section those animals have already been dealt with under the category of "all that is in the water.")

The Torah goes to great lengths to underscore the impurity of a *sheretz*. The Torah goes back and forth between the instructions not to eat them and descriptions of the impurity that they transfer.

There is a certain exception, however. In the laws of Leviticus, the Torah explains that flying "insects" are permitted for food if they have large jumping legs, and mentions by name four permitted types. Most Jewish communities seem to have lost interest in the tradition as to the identities of these species, although Yemenite Jewish communities have retained that knowledge.[69]

In practical terms, it is not likely in Western culture that one will have to turn down a dish of lizards or mice. Nonetheless, one important lesson from this passage is that gnats that drop into our soup are just as forbidden as camel-meat sandwiches, and we must abstain from both. See the chapter "Straining at Gnats" for more on this topic.

## Parts of the Animal

In order to keep biblically kosher, one must be mindful not only of the species of animal, but also the parts of the animal to be eaten. The first mention of a prohibited part of an animal occurs in Genesis 32:32. The chapter describes how the patriarch Jacob wrestled with a mysterious stranger until daybreak, until his opponent touched his hip, putting it out of joint. After that, the Torah explains, "Therefore to this day the people of Israel do not eat the sinew of the thigh that is on the hip socket, because he touched the socket of Jacob's hip on the sinew of the thigh." The Hebrew term for the "sinew of the thigh" (that is, the sciatic nerve) is *gid hanasheh* (גִּיד הַנָּשֶׁה).

Jewish commentators identify this as one of the 613 commandments of the Torah.[70] While this verse is not formulated as a command, the significance of this dietary practice is profound. Observance of this practice is identification with the struggle of Jacob, his overcoming, his blessing, and his new identity as Israel. Ignoring this custom would mean distancing oneself from each of these things, in which case eating kosher has little meaning.

Jewish tradition has retained the identity of the *gid hanasheh*, known today as the sciatic nerve. Completely removing this piece is a tedious surgical procedure. Nonetheless, there are some highly skilled individuals who are capable of doing so.

The Torah also indicates that the fat of certain animals is not to be eaten:

> It shall be a statute forever throughout your generations, in all your dwelling places, that you eat neither fat nor blood. (Leviticus 3:17)

> Speak to the people of Israel, saying, You shall eat no fat, of ox or sheep or goat. The fat of an animal that dies of itself and the fat of one that is torn by beasts may be put to any other use, but on no account shall you eat it. For every person who eats of the fat of an animal [Hebrew: *behemah*] of which a food offering may be made to the LORD shall be cut off from his people. (Leviticus 7:23–25)

It should be noted that the word translated "ox" (*shor*, שׁוֹר) actually has a much broader semantic range, including any bovine species, such as cows. (The term *behemah* is a more narrow term than its translation "animal," specifically referring to large land animals, meaning that other animals such as birds are not in view of this law.)

This would pose a problem for a literalist: How can one avoid eating any fat from an animal? All meat contains some amount of fat. At first glance, this law would preclude the possibility of eating any meat whatsoever.

Jewish interpretation sees the term for fat (*chelev*, חֵלֶב) in the context of the sacrificial laws, referring to fat portions and layers in the animal, rather than fat that is marbled into the meat. If meat is to be kosher, these fat portions must be selected out and removed. Rabbi Adin Steinsaltz defines *chelev* as:

> Animal fats prohibited by Torah law (in contrast to שׁוּמָן [*shumman*], which refers to permitted fats) ... Among the signs differentiating חֵלֶב [*chelev*] from שׁוּמָן [*shumman*] is the fact that חֵלֶב [*chelev*] lies above the meat and is not intertwined with it. It is enclosed by a thin membrane and is easily peeled away from the meat.[71]

As we will discuss in the next chapter, blood is also strictly forbidden. Some Jewish communities remove the larger blood vessels since they will contain blood.[72]

Much of the forbidden fat of an animal is found in the hindquarters. The blood vessels in the hindquarters are particularly difficult to remove. The sciatic nerve is also contained in the hindquarters. Considering all of these factors, many Jewish communities find that it is more cost-effective to sell the hindquarters to a non-kosher butcher. However, the meat contained in the hindquarters is not inherently non-kosher if it is properly processed by someone with the skill and knowledge to do so.

The forbidden portions of animals pose an equal challenge to biblical kosher as pure and impure species. If they do not come from a kosher slaughterhouse, ground beef, sausages, and hot dogs are guaranteed to contain these forbidden portions. To put it bluntly, typical ground meats sold at the local grocery store are not biblically kosher. Many meat cuts—especially those from the hindquarters such as tenderloin, T-bone, and filet mignon, as well as liver—are likely to contain forbidden parts of the animal as well. This is true regardless of whether or not the meat is labeled "organic," "natural," or "lean."

This means that while it is a worthwhile step forward to substitute beef sausage instead of pork pepperoni on a pizza, it still does not rise to the level of the Bible's kosher standard.

## Abstaining from Blood

The Torah prohibits the consumption of blood. It is surprising how many verses are dedicated to this prohibition. It is also remarkable how severely the Scriptures speak about the subject. It is called "a statute forever throughout your generations, in all your dwelling places" (Leviticus 3:17). One who eats blood is "cut off from his people," and God "sets his face against that person" (Leviticus 7:27; 17:10, 14). We must not eat it, so that "all may go well with you and with your children after you" (Deuteronomy 12:25).

The prohibition is not simply against drinking blood. The Torah indicates that animals that are slaughtered must be properly bled before the meat is eaten. The Scriptures tell us, "You shall not eat any flesh with the blood in it" (Leviticus 19:26). This law was even given to Noah, centuries earlier (Genesis 9:4). Instead, it repeatedly states that we should "pour it out on the earth like water," (Leviticus 17:13; Deuteronomy 12:16, 12:24, 15:23).

The Torah speaks of this in emphatic terms:

> Only be sure [literally, "be strong" (*chazak*, חֲזַק)] that you do not eat the blood, for the blood is the life, and you shall not eat the life with the flesh. (Deuteronomy 12:23)

How is one to be "strong" not to eat the blood with the flesh? At the very least this suggests that removing the blood from the slaughtered animal requires an intentional, concerted effort.

The Scriptures tell us the story of Saul's men, after striking down the Philistines:

> They struck down the Philistines that day from Michmash to Aijalon. And the people were very faint. The people pounced on the spoil and took sheep and oxen and calves and slaughtered them on the ground. And the people ate them with the blood. Then they told Saul, "Behold, the people are sinning against the LORD by eating with the blood." And he said, "You have dealt treacherously;

roll a great stone to me here." And Saul said, "Disperse yourselves among the people and say to them, 'Let every man bring his ox or his sheep and slaughter them here and eat, and do not sin against the LORD by eating with the blood.'" So every one of the people brought his ox with him that night and they slaughtered them there. (1 Samuel 14:31–34)

These men were not drinking the blood as a beverage. They were not pagans; they were just being careless, slaughtering the animals in an improper way ("on the ground") that did not allow the blood to drain.

The idea that there is a certain way that animals must be slaughtered can be found in the Torah:

> If the place that the LORD your God will choose to put his name there is too far from you, then you may kill [Hebrew: *zavach*] any of your herd or your flock, which the LORD has given you, as I have commanded you, and you may eat within your towns whenever you desire. (Deuteronomy 12:21)

"Kill" is an imprecise choice of words in this translation. The Hebrew term *zavach* (זָבַח) specifically means "slaughter," and it is frequently used in regards to sacrifices.

This clause implies a prescribed method of slaughter. The text's use of the verb *zavach*, which refers to sacrificial slaughter, indicates that secular slaughter is to be performed by the method used in sacrificial slaughter, namely slitting the animal's throat.[73]

How are we to slaughter an animal "as I have commanded you"? This suggests that a proper method of slaughter was demonstrated to the ancient Israelites.[74]

There are explicit parameters around the method of the animal's death. The Torah states:

> You shall be consecrated to me. Therefore you shall not eat any flesh that is torn by beasts in the field; you shall throw it to the dogs. (Exodus 22:31)

> You shall not eat anything that has died naturally. (Deuteronomy 14:21)

The translation of Deuteronomy 14:21 is somewhat loose. Literally, the text reads, "You shall not eat any carcass." Since we cannot eat a live animal, any animal we eat will be a carcass at some point. For this reason, the translators felt the necessity of providing further interpretation. However, it is important to note that it is irrelevant whether the animal died of natural or unnatural causes. Thus, this verse instructs that someone must have killed the animal in an acceptable way, whatever that is. If an animal did not die in the proper manner, then the animal is not kosher, regardless of whether or not the blood has been drained from the carcass.

We should also consider the four apostolic injunctions upon Gentiles, which includes the instruction to abstain from "what has been strangled" (Acts 15:20, 15:29, 21:25).

While the term "strangle" in English specifically denotes death by constriction around the neck or windpipe, the Greek term (*pniktos*, πνικτός) has a broader definition which includes choking, suffocation, and asphyxiation, not merely strangling. For example, the Gospel of Mark uses a form of this word to describe the demon-possessed pigs that were "drowned" in the sea (Mark 5:13).

The term *pniktos* is the Greek equivalent of the Hebrew term for "choke" (*chanak*, חָנַק). This Hebrew word is a technical term in traditional kosher law. The Mishnah (m.*Chullin* 1:2) explains that dull blades or cutting instruments cannot be used in kosher slaughter, since the blood will then enter the animal's windpipe, thus "choking" the animal. Rather than dying of blood loss (as seems to be the Torah's intention) the animal dies of asphyxiation, rendering it "strangled." This use of the term *pniktos* can also be found in Philo's writings.[75]

Several scholars make the case that the apostolic prohibition of "what has been strangled" thus refers to improperly slaughtered animals.

> "Strangled meat" referred to animals that had been slaughtered in a manner that left the blood in it. Blood was considered sacred to Jews, and all meat was to be drained of blood before consuming it.[76]

> "What has been strangled," i.e., meat from animals improperly or not ritually butchered, without having

the blood drained from them (Leviticus 17:15 cf. 7:24; Exodus 22:31).[77]

"Strangled meat," i.e., meat from animals not slaughtered by pouring out their blood, in conformity with biblical and Jewish practice.[78]

Bauckham explains the significance of the term used in Acts and its relationship with Leviticus:

"Things strangled" (πνικτων) are prohibited in Leviticus 17:13. The difficulty with this term in the apostolic decree has arisen simply because Leviticus 17:13 is a positive prescription: that animals killed for eating must be slaughtered in such a way that their blood drains out. Abstention from πνικτων is the negative collar, for an animal killed in such a way that the blood remains "choked."[79]

Although the Torah does not explicitly describe the proper method of slaughter, traditional kosher slaughter is done in such a way that the major blood vessels in the neck are cut with a sharp knife, without damaging the windpipe. That way, the animal's death is almost painless, and the heart continues to pump the blood out of the body until the animal falls asleep.

One cannot prove purely from biblical text that this is the only proper method of slaughter. Nonetheless, at the very least we can see that the method of death and the method of slaughter are significant in terms of biblical kosher law. We would do well to investigate whether or not other killing and butchering methods meet this standard.

When animals are slaughtered according to USDA regulations, they are first stunned (rendered unconscious), and only then is the animal cut and bled. The USDA highly discourages bleeding without stunning, as is required by traditional kosher law. Stunning is performed in any of the following ways: a) a mechanical blow to the brain, b) electrical shock, or c) gassing with either carbon dioxide or a combination of inert gases.[80] According to World Organisation for Animal Health, the electrical shock method is sometimes performed in a way that causes cardiac arrest.[81]

Animals that are hunted for food are subject to more issues. These animals are frequently in a stressed condition at the time of death. Their muscles clench and their bodies are surging with adrenalin, which may inhibit the draining of blood. Their death may be slow and painful, and there may be considerable time between killing and bleeding the animal.[82]

In defining death, we must also consider the differences in perspective between biblical law, civil law, and modern science. While civil law and modern science may define death as a cessation of brain activity or cardiac arrest, the Bible seems to draw a connection between life and breathing. That is to say, a biblical definition of death appears to be when breathing ceases.[83] Thus, there may be a point at which the USDA considers the animal to be alive, although biblically the animal may already be dead.

Does the typical USDA method of slaying animals meet the biblical standard? The Jewish community has concluded decisively that it does not.

## Purging Vessels

Another aspect of kosher law can be found in the book of Numbers. After the war of vengeance against the Midianites, the Israelite soldiers were not allowed to enter the Israelite camp until they went through a process of purification. The spoils they carried home from the war also had to be cleansed before they could be brought into the Israelite camp.

Then Eleazar the priest said to the men in the army who had gone to battle,

> This is the statute of the law that the LORD has commanded Moses: only the gold, the silver, the bronze, the iron, the tin, and the lead, everything that can stand the fire, you shall pass through the fire, and it shall be clean. Nevertheless, it shall also be purified with the water for impurity. And whatever cannot stand the fire, you shall pass through the water. (Numbers 31:21–23)

One aspect of this translation is misleading. Rather than "everything that can stand the fire," a more literal translation would be "everything that goes into the fire." Likewise, "whatever cannot stand the fire" is more literally rendered, "everything that does not go in the fire."

The reason this is significant is that the translation, as it stands, seems to imply that everything *ideally* should be purified in a fire, but if the fire would damage it, ritual washing is good enough. However, this is not consistent with ritual purity laws elsewhere, in which if the object cannot be properly purified, it is simply destroyed.[84] However, if we simply read the passage literally, it seems to speak of objects that are used in fire (such as pots and pans) as opposed to those that are not. As Rashi comments, "'Everything that goes into the fire,' that is, in order to cook something in it."[85]

That is to say, if the object was contaminated in a fire, then it must also be cleansed in a fire. If the object had not been contaminated in a fire, a cleansing with fire is not necessary. This reading brings clarity and consistency to the laws revealed in this passage.

### Levitical purity?

One might claim that this commandment refers only to ritual purity that is separate from kosher law and only practical in the context of Temple ritual. However, we can see that this is not the case, since "everything that goes into the fire" must first be cleansed in fire, making it "clean" and then also "purified" in water. If a fire-purged vessel is somehow "clean" and yet also "impure," then we must be speaking of two separate concepts. There is nowhere else in the Torah where ritual purity is effected by passing though fire. Ramban explains,

> A vessel that touches a deceased person or a carcass is not made ritually pure with fire, since the only immersion in the Torah is with water. Thus, our sages were required to explain that this purification is for the purpose of purging them from forbidden foods that they absorbed in the possession of Gentiles.[86]

If the purity achieved here is strictly Tabernacle-related, then that would indicate that pots and bowls made of tin and lead could go from the Midianite dinner table to the Israelite priesthood. This makes little sense. Even the gold and silver vessels would probably have been melted down and re-formed into the specialized dishes needed for Levitical purposes.

Additionally, notice that this command of purification is directed to "the men in the army who had gone to battle" (Numbers 31:21). This description automatically excludes all priests and Levites, since they do not go out to battle.[87] If these dishes are only being purified because they are to be devoted to sacred use, then what is the purpose of giving this commandment to soldiers? The plain reading of the text suggests that these dishes were among the plunder that was divided "into two parts between the warriors who went out to battle and all the congregation" (Numbers 31:27).

Jewish tradition explains the "passing through fire" as communicating that the flavors and particles of non-kosher food are transmitted through heat, and they can only be purged through the same level of heat.[88]

This interpretation is borne out by modern knowledge. Consider, for example, a cast iron skillet. To season the skillet in a conventional manner, one might coat the pan with lard or bacon grease, and then bake the pan in an oven. The only way to remove the seasoning would be with intense heat.

A similar effect occurs in the inside of an oven. *Wired Magazine* recently published an article explaining why New York pizza is so much better than pizza in San Francisco. The answer was explained by David Tisi, whom *Wired* describes as "a food-development consultant who has spent much of his career studying pizza."

> "As you cook, some ingredients vaporize, and these volatilized particles can attach themselves to the walls of the baking cavity," Tisi says. "The next time you use the oven, these bits get caught up in the convection currents and deposited on the food, which adds flavor." Over time, he says, more particles join the mix and mingle with the savory soot from burned wood or coal — the only fuels worth using — to create a flavor that you can't grow in a garden: gestalt, if you will.[89]

Another illustration of the contamination of vessels can be seen among individuals with severe and sensitive allergies. Many people with allergies have severe reactions after eating foods if they were prepared on the same equipment that was used with allergens, even if the equipment is thoroughly cleaned.

Imagine if you were fatally allergic to pork, and the slightest amount would threaten your life. If this were the case, would you be comfortable eating fish that was seared on a grill in an Americana restaurant, served on a stoneware plate? Non-kosher food can be seen to affect us in a similar way, only it is detrimental to our souls rather than our bodies.

Even if the end goal of the cleansing in fire in this passage is entirely ritual, it makes sense that it would only be possible to cleanse something ritually after it has been completely cleansed hygienically. In other words, immersing a pan in water to remove ritual impurity is only possible after all traces of non-kosher food have been removed. A vessel does not qualify for ritual purification if it still contains contaminating substances (such as unclean species and pagan sacrifices). Immersing it would be as ineffective as taking a ritual bath while holding onto a dead rat. That means that a hygienic cleansing is the prerequisite and first stage of a ritual cleansing process.

In the world today, without a Temple, priesthood, or sacrifices, some people believe that ritual purity has absolutely no practical bearing on life. That belief is not shared by traditional Judaism.

While it is not explicit in the text, traditional Judaism sees the second purification—the washing in water—as related not to the holiness of the Tabernacle but of the entire Israelite nation. The vessels go through a rededication ceremony. They were originally formed by Midianites for the purpose of containing food offered to idols and celebrating pagan feasts. But now, as they enter Jewish homes, they are devoted to a new, holier purpose: the service of the one true God. It is as if the dishes themselves are "baptized" and undergo a religious conversion. This idea is supported by the special role of the Jewish people as "a kingdom of priests and a holy nation" (Exodus 19:6).

Nonetheless, if the ritual purity of these vessels was not an issue, then that would only account for the second purification in water, since the first purification in fire is hygienic. For the purposes of dietary law alone, there is still a need to cleanse the vessel of all traces of contaminants, and the process that the Torah prescribes for this is "passing through a fire."

Perhaps you are not convinced that this is the original intent of Numbers 31:21–23. That is understandable, since the passage is short on details. Nonetheless, a law of the Torah is revealed here; the passage has to have some meaning. If we dismiss the traditional explanation, then it becomes our duty to propose another, which must also account for the double cleansing of verse 23. The traditional Jewish explanation is, at the very least, both biblical and reasonable.

## "Kashering" to Remove Holiness

There is another text that we may bring to bear on the issue of cleansing vessels. This passage is different, however, because instead of imparting holiness to vessels, the task is to remove it.

> The LORD spoke to Moses, saying, "Speak to Aaron and his sons, saying, This is the law of the sin offering. In the place where the burnt offering is killed shall the sin offering be killed before the LORD; it is most holy. The priest who offers it for sin shall eat it. In a holy place it shall be eaten, in the court of the tent of meeting. Whatever touches its flesh shall be holy, and when any of its blood is splashed on a garment, you shall wash that on which it was splashed in a holy place. And the earthenware vessel in which it is boiled shall be broken. But if it is boiled in a bronze vessel, that shall be scoured and rinsed in water. Every male among the priests may eat of it; it is most holy. But no sin offering shall be eaten from which any blood is brought into the tent of meeting to make atonement in the Holy Place; it shall be burned up with fire." (Leviticus 6:17–23[24–30])

This passage is puzzling. Why must the vessel in which the offering was boiled be either cleansed or destroyed?

One explanation is that holy or consecrated foods can only be eaten by certain individuals, in a state of ritual purity, under specific circumstances (which vary). Now imagine that someone cooked sacrificial meat in an earthenware pot. The priest is very careful to prepare himself ritually before partaking of this meat.

The following day, however, the priest sits down to enjoy a non-sanctified meal of boiled vegetables. But since he used the same earthenware pot that he had used for the sacrificial meat, the flavor of the holy food becomes infused into the vegetables. The remaining particles of the sacrifices are considered leftovers from the sacrifice, which are not kosher (Leviticus 7:16–18).

The Torah seeks to prevent this by requiring that the dishes in which the meat was cooked be purged of the flavor of the holy meat. In the case of earthenware, this is not possible, so the dish must be broken to prevent the dish from being used again. The sages derive from this that earthenware in which non-kosher foods have been cooked cannot be made kosher again because the flavor can never be fully removed.[90]

## Meat and Dairy

Three times in the Torah the instruction is repeated, "You shall not boil a young goat in its mother's milk" (Exodus 23:19, 34:26; Deuteronomy 14:21). This commandment is carried over into traditional Jewish practice as a complete separation of all meat and dairy products.

This issue is often taken to exemplify the difference between "biblical" and "rabbinic" kosher. The difference between the English translation of the verse and normative kosher law is so stark that many people perceive it as a classic example of a non-biblical rabbinic ruling.

It is no secret that rabbinical rulings exist that go beyond mere interpretation of the Torah. Jewish scholars refer to these rulings as *derabbanan* (דְּרַבָּנָן), which means "of our rabbis," in contrast with the laws that are *de'oraita* (דְּאֹורָיְתָא), meaning "of the Torah." The difference between these two types of laws is an important distinction in Judaism.

Rabbinic rulings are set in place for various reasons, the most common being in order to prevent the likely transgression of a biblical law. Often those reasons are misunderstood, and sometimes they might seem like a stretch to us, but regardless, the explanation for these rulings can be found. (Such is not the case in biblical law, on the other hand. More often than not, the Scriptures are silent in regards to the meaning and purpose they were given, leaving us only to ponder and speculate.)

One might think that the sages instituted an additional law separating meat and dairy as just such a buffer. It would seem that the intention of separating the two was to prevent a scenario in which a young goat might actually be boiled in the milk of its mother. However, the sages do not see the separation of meat and dairy as an additional "fence" at all.[91] Rather, this law is considered "biblical" in its very essence. The sages seem to have felt that the separation of meat and dairy arises from the text itself. (In fact, they do not seem to even know for certain why God prohibited the combination.)

Somehow, the elders and teachers in Israel thousands of years ago read the same verses in Hebrew and concluded that God had instructed us not to serve meat and dairy together. How is that possible?

So far we have found that although the English translation is often helpful, it also quite often leads us off course. We have run across Hebrew words translated into English words with a much broader meaning,[92] as well as those translated into English words with a narrower meaning.[93] We have found words that are roughly equivalent but do not match a modern scientific definition.[94] There have been cases where the translators felt a need to supply words that were missing,[95] as well as cases where they interpreted a passage for us, although their interpretation may not have been correct.[96] We have even found that a literal, non-interpretive translation can lead us astray when it is not taken in its proper context.[97] This goes to show that to understand the Bible we must read it in its original language and familiarize ourselves with the culture and interpretation that surrounds it.

If we examine this commandment in light of the original language and culture, we will at least make some steps in bridging the gap between the historic Jewish interpretation and the modern English translation we have been given.

## You Shall Not Boil

The instruction begins by saying, "You shall not boil." If we were to accept this translation at face value and take a hyper-literal approach to the commandment, we might find it perfectly acceptable to place a young goat in a pot of its mother's milk and heat it to 211 degrees Fahrenheit, just below the boiling point. Since it did not reach a full 212 degrees, it did not technically boil.[98] Or perhaps we would feel comfortable at an even higher temperature if we employed a different cooking method, for example, if it were fried or baked instead of boiled.

Of course, to be that literal is to place a lot of faith in our translation of the Hebrew as "boil." We would have to bank on the idea that the Hebrew term translated "boil" here has the exact same range of meaning.

The Hebrew verb we translate as "boil" is *bishel* (בִּשֵׁל).[99] There are times when "boil" seems like a fair and reasonable translation. There are other times when it cannot possibly mean "boil." (In the Scriptural quotations below, **bold** text indicates the translation of the Hebrew word *bishel*.)

One example where it does mean "boil" is in the commandment of the Passover lamb:

> They shall eat the flesh that night, roasted on the fire; with unleavened bread and bitter herbs they shall eat it. Do not eat any of it raw or **boiled** [*uvashel mevushal*, וּבָשֵׁל מְבֻשָּׁל], in water, but roasted, its head with its legs and its inner parts. (Exodus 12:8–9)

We can see from this verse that the Passover lamb cannot be boiled; it must only be roasted. However, we find elsewhere,

> You may not offer the Passover sacrifice within any of your towns that the LORD your God is giving you, but at the place that the LORD your God will choose, to make his name dwell in it, there you shall offer the Passover sacrifice, in the evening at sunset, at the time you came out of Egypt. **And you shall cook it** [*uvishalta*, וּבִשַּׁלְתָּ] and eat it at the place that the LORD your God will choose. And in the morning you shall turn and go to your tents. (Deuteronomy 16:5–7)

In this case, the translators were aware of the discrepancy, so they (appropriately) chose the more generic term "cook" rather than "boil." And yet the term is the same.

In the account of the celebration of Passover during the reign of Josiah, we find a similar usage:

> **And they roasted** [*vayevashelu*, וַיְבַשְׁלוּ] the Passover lamb with fire according to the rule; and **they boiled** [*bishelu*, בִּשְּׁלוּ] the holy offerings in pots, in cauldrons, and in pans, and carried them quickly to all the lay people. (2 Chronicles 35:13)

Here we find the same term[100] translated both as "roasted" and "boiled" in the same sentence. (In Exodus 12:8–9 cited above, however, the word translated "roasted" [*tzali*, צָלִי] is entirely different.)

Yet another use of the term can be found:

> So Tamar went to her brother Amnon's house, where he was lying down. And she took dough and kneaded it and made cakes in his sight **and baked** [*vatevashel*, וַתְּבַשֵּׁל] the cakes. (2 Samuel 13:8)

Between all of these uses ("boil," "cook," "roast," and "bake"), it seems fair to say that the verb *bishel* does not necessarily mean "boil" in a technical, scientific sense. Rather, its versatility is comparable to the English word "cook." The Theological Wordbook of the Old Testament defines the root word as "seethe, bake, boil, roast, and grow ripe."[101]

As with the word "cook," it certainly suggests that heat is applied. But even so, that might not even be the point. Consider if someone were to say, "My husband will be able to eat with us, as long as you don't cook anything with tomatoes." In this case, "cook" is not the operative word, and the listener would most likely assume that raw tomatoes are as bad as cooked. Likewise, we might say that a person is "cooking" even if they are tossing a green salad, since the point is not the heat involved but the food preparation.[102]

If we stick to the interpretation of *bishel* as cooking with heat, then we must ask the question of how much heat constitutes "cooking." And would it really be acceptable to serve a young goat in its mother's milk if the goat had been pre-cooked elsewhere first?

After all, if we were to take this word hyper-literally, it would be entirely permissible to *eat* a young goat boiled in its mother's milk, if someone else did the preparing, since technically the text does not say, "You shall not eat." But the sages naturally concluded that cooking and eating are both prohibited.

So far, we have shown that the verse prohibits *cooking* a young goat in its mother's milk. We also must consider that the amount of heat may not be relevant.

Before we continue, I should explain my use of hypothetical situations. I am not suggesting that anyone should or would actually pre-cook a young goat and then serve it in its mother's milk. The purpose of these hypothetical situations is simply to explore the complete parameters of the law at hand. If we are to accuse the traditional interpretation of the commandment of being too broad in scope, then it becomes our duty to define the exact boundary between right and wrong.

## A Young Goat

The next term to consider is the word translated "a young goat." The Hebrew word is *gedi* (גְּדִי).

The English phrase "a young goat" is quite specific. If we assume our translation has razor-sharp precision, then it should be perfectly acceptable to cook a young lamb in its mother's milk.

The term *gedi* is used a total of sixteen times in the Hebrew Scriptures, including the three verses that contain the commandment not to cook a *gedi* in its mother's milk. Ten of the remaining thirteen instances (including all of the other instances in the five books of the Torah) occur in a two-word construct: "a *gedi* of goats" (*gedi izzim*, גְּדִי־עִזִּים).

If *gedi* only means "young goat," then what would be the point of modifying the word *gedi* with the specific term "of goats"? The fact that the phrase "a *gedi* of goats" is so common indicates that *gedi* alone would not necessarily refer to a goat in specific.

When we look at the other three passages in which *gedi* stands alone,[103] we find that in these cases the exact species of animal is not of great consequence.

If the exact animal species was important in the case of cooking in its mother's milk, we would have expected the Torah to use the specific form. The fact that in this commandment the Torah deviates from the conventional construct in order to leave *gedi* unmodified shows that the species of the animal is not the main concern. It seems that this word was chosen to refer to the young of any livestock. The *Shulchan Aruch* explains,

> *Gedi* is not specific terminology, as this law applies to cattle, sheep, and goats. The term *gedi* includes the young of cattle, the young of a sheep, and the young of a goat. This is why the text specifies "*gedi* of goats" in passages such as, "Judah sent the *gedi* of goats" (Genesis 38:20) and, "... the skins of the *gedayim* of goats" in order to indicate goats specifically. But in any place where it says *gedi* alone, cattle and sheep are included (see b.*Chullin* 113a).[104]

The Greek of the *LXX* supports a loose interpretation as well. In each of the three instances of this commandment in the Torah, the *LXX* renders the Hebrew word *gedi* as the Greek *aren* (αρήν), which does not mean "kid" but "lamb."[105] Likewise, Philo of Alexandria assumes the prohibition applies to cattle, sheep, and goats.[106] Thus Jacob Milgrom writes,

> Is it, then, so farfetched for the rabbis to have deduced that all meat, not just of the kid, and all milk, not only of the mother, may not be served together? The interpretation is clearly an old one. It is already adumbrated in the third century BCE.[107]

But if "goat" is not the point of the verse, why did the Torah choose the term *gedi*, a word that is frequently paired with goats?

To understand this, let's consider one of the ways in which the culture of the Ancient Near East was different from our own. In our world, cows are the main producers of milk for drinking. It is rare that milk would come from any other source. When someone just says "milk," they nearly always mean cow milk. If you were to ask a child, "Where does milk come from?" the answer would likely be "cows," even though a more complete answer is "mammals."

Suppose your friend said, "I never drink milk if the cows were treated with antibiotics." What if your friend was offered milk from a goat that was treated with antibiotics instead? Your friend would probably not want it either. Your friend only mentioned cows because they are the most common source of milk.

In the Ancient Near East, milk from cows was rarely used for drinking. Vamosh writes, "Goats, therefore, and to a lesser extent sheep, were a much more common source of milk than cows."[108] When someone thought of milk, they thought of goats, not cows. Nathan MacDonald explains,

> This association is clear in the rabbinic period; Rabbi Nachman is reported to have said, "a goat for its milk, a ewe for its fleece … oxen for ploughing." The association of milk with goats can already be found in the Old Testament: a kid must not be cooked in its mother's milk (Deut. 14:21), and according to Proverbs 27:26–27, "lambs will provide your clothing, and male goats the price of a field; there will be enough goats' milk for your food." The reason for preferring goats to sheep is clear enough. Sheep have about half the annual milk yield of goats, and lactate for about three months, while goats can be milked for up to five months.[109]

For someone who lives in a culture that strongly associates milk with goats, it would be perfectly natural to use the term *gedi* in place of any milk-producing animal. This is especially true because *gedi* can refer to other animals as well as goats. Because of this, the term that might be understood in a specific sense nonetheless stands in for the general category.[110]

But what about the "young" aspect of *gedi*? Would it really be permissible to cook a mature goat in its mother's milk? After all, it would not be uncommon to find a goat that still produced milk and had mature offspring.

But again, animals were typically slaughtered for meat while they were still young. It makes sense to refer to butchered animals in general as "younglings," just as it is natural to refer to motor vehicles in general as "cars."

All animals were young at some point. The use of a term that implies youth could possibly serve more of a purpose relating to the symbolic significance of the prohibition, rather than to denote an age limit.

Can we take a commandment that sounds so specific and expand it to something general? As it was shown, the original Hebrew words already support a broader interpretation. In addition, this could be considered one of several laws in which a specific instance is used to illustrate a general principle.

For example, the Torah speaks of an ox that gores a person:

> When an ox gores a man or a woman to death, the ox shall be stoned, and its flesh shall not be eaten, but the owner of the ox shall not be liable. (Exodus 21:28)

But what if a person was gored by a ram or goat? Suppose it was a dog that bit him. Since the Torah is silent regarding these species, is there no recourse for the victim?

Rather, here is a prime example of a type of law in the Torah where a specific example is cited to illustrate a general principle. The point of this law is not the type of animal involved, but an ox was chosen as an example because it represents a typical case. Rashi comments on this verse,

> It does not matter whether the animal is an ox or any beast, animal or bird. The verse is merely speaking about what is typical.[111]

Finally, the phrase "boil a young goat in its mother's milk" might evoke the mental image of a whole animal lying in the pot. But had a dish such as this been served, the goat would have been fully slaughtered and processed, leaving not "a goat" in the pot but small cuts of goat meat.

Thus, we can see how the term *gedi*, in the context of this verse, could reasonably be understood as "meat." So far, we can see that it is reasonable to interpret the verse as "you shall not *cook meat* in its mother's milk."

### In the Milk

Our English translation reads, "in its mother's milk," but the word order in Hebrew is more like "in the milk of its mother," so let's deal with "in the milk" first and then "of its mother" afterward.

First off, the word translated "in" is a simple one-letter prefix (*be*, בְּ). One might think that boiling the goat meat immersed in its mother's milk would be prohibited, but adding a small amount of milk to a meat dish would be acceptable. However, the preposition *be* has a broad range of meanings, including "in," "on," and "with." It would be equally accurate to translate "with its mother's milk" instead of "in its mother's milk."

Next, we should discuss the idea of "milk." Sure, cooking a young goat in its mother's milk is prohibited, but what about if the milk has been processed into yogurt or cheese? Does the prohibition apply only to the type of milk we get in cartons at the grocery store, or does it apply to all kinds of dairy?

The word translated "milk" here is *chalav* (חָלָב). Vamosh seems to have a different idea about what this term means:

> Not all biblical translations agree on the meaning of the Hebrew words for the various milk products in Scripture. In its simplest form, the Hebrew word *chalav* could simply mean milk as we know it. But in the hot climate of the Holy Land, this liquid would not have remained fresh for long.[112]

In the Ancient Near East, it seems likely that nearly all milk was processed and fermented into a form that could be used over longer periods of time.

Nathan MacDonald writes,

> It is difficult to judge whether biblical references to *chalab*, the word usually translated "milk," are to be understood as fresh milk or processed dairy products.[113]

In modern Hebrew, *chalav* can mean "milk" specifically, but it can also refer to "dairy" in general. For example, cheese that is produced with only Jews involved in the production is labeled *chalav Yisra'el* (חָלָב יִשְׂרָאֵל).

But this is not simply a modern Hebrew phenomenon. The broad semantic range of the word *chalav* can be seen in the Tanach:

> Also take these ten cheeses to the commander of their thousand. See if your brothers are well, and bring some token from them. (1 Samuel 17:18)

The term translated "cheeses" here is the Hebrew *charitzei he-chalav* (חָרִצֵי הֶחָלָב), very literally translated, "the cuts of milk."

Accordingly, the Theological Wordbook of the Old Testament defines *chalav* as "milk, sour milk, cheese," and comments,

> Because of the warm climate, people of the Near East generally utilized the milk not as milk or butter, but as sour milk or curds (yogurt).[114]

Thus, any dairy food can be considered *chalav*. This means that it would not be permissible to boil a young goat in its mother's yogurt or melt a slice of cheese made from the mother's milk on a cut of meat. We can now interpret the verse, "You shall not *cook meat with* its mother's *dairy*."

### Of Its Mother

Finally, we are presented with the phrase "its mother," which in Hebrew is *immo* (אִמּוֹ).

Hebrew frequently uses familial terms in an idiomatic sense. Quite frequently, words like "brother," "father," "son," and "daughter" are used in a different way from their literal meaning. In Hebrew, "brother" can refer to a person's "kinsman," "countryman," or "friend." "Father" can be used to speak of a "source" or "originator." "Son" is a way to say that a person is characterized by something (such as a "son of peace"). "Daughters" can mean "women" or "inhabitants." Thus, there is a real possibility that the familial relationship spoken of here is also idiomatic. However, the main difficulty with a face-value translation of this term is practical, rather than linguistic.

Imagine you were the owner of a large flock of goats in ancient Israel. At a given time, you had several goats giving milk. After milking each of your goats, would you have kept each goat's milk in separate, labeled containers? Will you have a warehouse full of jugs labeled "Bessy," "Henrietta," "Stella," "Millie," and "Sugarplum"? How would you tell one goat's milk from the next? First of all, once the milk is removed from the goat, it is indistinguishable from any other milk. Second, all of your goats' milk would be pooled into one place.

If a man had only one goat, then he would not be able to cook any of its young in milk, since the milk would be from that one goat. If a man had two or more goats, the milk would be combined together into a single vessel, and still none of it could be used to cook with the young goats.

On the one hand, the Torah specifically mentions the milk "of its mother." On the other hand, one would have to go out of his way to separate out milk that came from a particular animal. The original livestock owners who received this law would find themselves in a situation where they were unable to use any of their milk to cook with meat. But as a result, the phrase "of its mother" served no practical purpose to the people who first saw the Torah. To them, it might as well have just said, "in milk." Thus leaves us to ask if "of its mother" might have a meaning beyond its face value.

The sages dealt with this question, and one conclusion is that the phrase "its mother's milk" teaches us that the prohibition only applies to animals of a species that gives milk.

In Deuteronomy 14:21, the prohibition of the *gedi* with dairy comes immediately after the commandment, "You shall not eat anything that has died naturally." The sages saw the first law as context for the second. That is to say, the types of animals that would be prohibited if they died naturally must be the same types of animal described by *gedi*. This would include a variety of animals, including even birds.

But the Torah continues by saying "in *its mother's* milk" to limit the scope of the law only to animals that provide milk for human consumption, such as cows, sheep, and goats. In other words, we must not cook the meat of a dairy species in the milk of a dairy species. According to the Mishnah, this technically excludes poultry, wild animals, and non-kosher animals from the prohibition.[115]

Bringing this perspective into our interpretive translation, we should then limit the type of meat involved only to that of dairy livestock: cows, sheep, and goats. Thus, the passage could be translated, "You shall not cook beef, lamb, or goat with dairy."

## Poultry with Dairy

Even though the biblical commandment specifically limits the prohibition to animals that give milk, the sages saw fit to extend the prohibition also to poultry. This is a case where we can draw a clear line of distinction between biblical and rabbinic kosher laws. Whereas the prohibition of cooking red meat with dairy arises directly from the biblical text, the sages openly admit that the separation of poultry from dairy is a rabbinic safeguard.[116] Although there is dispute in the Talmud about the separation of poultry from dairy,[117] the rabbinic prohibition is almost universally observed throughout the Jewish world. (There is no dispute, however, about the separation of red meat from dairy.)

Thus, one who keeps red meat separate from dairy but chooses to combine poultry with dairy can legitimately claim to observe biblical kosher laws.

But to be fair, the idea of safeguarding the *Torah* is biblical as well. The Hebrew word *shamar* (שמר), often translated "keep" (as in "keep the commandments"), literally means "protect." A literal translation of Proverbs 7:2 says, "protect my commandments and live; [protect] my Torah like [it is] the pupil of your eye." Of sin, personified as an adulterous woman, it says, "do not stray into her paths" (Proverbs 7:25). "Whoever keeps the commandment keeps his life" (Proverbs 19:16).

## Ancient Practice

One might ask: is the separation of meat and dairy an ancient custom? Was this the original interpretation of the passage, or did it develop later? Specifically, was this the custom in the first century, and would our master Yeshua have interpreted it that way?

### Mishnah

This interpretation was already firmly in place at the time that the Mishnah was codified (c. 200 CE).[118] Hillel and Shammai were famous sages who lived in the generation just prior to our master Yeshua. The school of Hillel had a reputation for being more lenient than the school of Shammai in most areas of Jewish law. On the separation of meat and dairy, however, Hillel was more strict than Shammai, prohibiting even the placing of poultry and dairy on the same table. (Shammai prohibited placing red meat and dairy on the same table and eating poultry with dairy, but he allowed poultry to be on the same table as dairy.) There are numerous parallels between Hillel and our master Yeshua, and his rulings overwhelmingly seem to match those of Hillel.

The schools of Hillel and Shammai differed on many points of Jewish law, but on the basics of meat and dairy, they are in complete agreement. Both held that red meat and dairy must be kept separate as a matter of biblical law, and poultry and dairy must be kept separate as a matter of rabbinic law. The fact that these two schools agreed on these points suggests that the interpretation pre-dates the division of the two schools, placing it at least as early as the beginning of the first century CE.

Rabbi Adin Steinsaltz writes:

> The biblical passage "Thou shalt not cook the kid in its mother's milk" (Exodus 23:19) was understood from very ancient times, and, at least in the middle of the Second Temple era, as a ban on cooking any animal flesh in milk. Over the centuries it was extended until (from about the time of the Houses of Hillel and Shammai) it encompassed birds as well.[119]

### Targumim

Another helpful source of information is the *targumim*. The *targumim* are ancient translations of the Hebrew Scriptures into Aramaic. They were used alongside the Hebrew in places where Aramaic was better understood. These translations were quite interpretive, making them more of a commentary or exposition. This is helpful because it teaches us some of the scriptural interpretations that were common at the time that the *targumim* were written.

The most famous of the *targumim* on the Torah is *Targum Onkelos*. This targum is attributed to a man named Onkelos[120] (or Aquilas in Greek), who lived about 35–120 CE.[121]

As far as *targumim* go, Onkelos tends to be more literal than most. Yet, note how Onkelos translates the passages in question:

| English Standard Version | Targum Onkelos [122] |
|---|---|
| The best of the firstfruits of your ground you shall bring into the house of the LORD your God. You shall not boil a young goat in its mother's milk. (Exodus 23:19) | The beginning of the first fruits of thy land thou shalt bring into the sanctuary of the Lord thy God. Thou shalt not eat flesh with milk. |
| The best of the firstfruits of your ground you shall bring to the house of the LORD your God. You shall not boil a young goat in its mother's milk. (Exodus 34:26) | The chief of the firstfruits of thy land thou shalt bring to the sanctuary of the Lord thy God. Thou shalt not eat flesh with milk. |
| You shall not eat anything that has died naturally. You may give it to the sojourner who is within your towns, that he may eat it, or you may sell it to a foreigner. For you are a people holy to the LORD your God. You shall not boil a young goat in its mother's milk. (Deuteronomy 14:21) | You shall not eat of any thing that dieth of itself: thou mayest give it to the uncircumcised stranger who is in thy city, and he may eat it; or thou mayest sell it to the outward people; for thou art to be a holy people to the Lord thy God. Thou shalt not eat flesh with the milk. |

## Samaritans

Samaritans are an example of a group well outside the realm of rabbinic interpretation.[123] Their appearances in the Gospels frequently reflect the state of hostility between the Samaritans and the Jewish community. And yet, Samaritans also practice the separation of meat and dairy.

Reinhard Pummer describes Samaritan practice this way:

> The consumption of meat and milk together is forbidden. As in Judaism, the prohibition is deduced from Exod 23:19 (34:26; Deut 14:21). It is briefly mentioned in the eleventh century halakhic works as well as in the *Hillukh*.[124]

The fact that Samaritans observe this prohibition suggests that it is of ancient origin, since Samaritan practice originated at the time of the first exile.

## No Dairy Offerings

The Torah repeatedly praises the land of Israel by speaking of it as a "land flowing with milk and honey," even during the declaration of first fruits, as a person brings gifts from their harvest to God.[125] One would expect that since milk was something that symbolized the bounty of the land, it would be prescribed as an offering in the Temple. Fruit, grain, oil, and meat were presented before God, but why do we not find milk, cheese, or other dairy offerings?

It is possible that dairy was not brought into the Tabernacle to prevent the combination of meat and dairy. If this is true, then the separation of meat and dairy dates back to the Torah itself.

## Yeshua and Separation of Meat and Dairy

Did our master Yeshua separate meat and dairy? Consider these factors:

- Separation of meat and dairy was standard practice in the first century.
- The Master never raises any objection to the separation of meat and dairy.
- His contemporaries never accused him of eating meat and dairy together, even though in the Talmudic era combining poultry with dairy (let alone red meat) was enough to merit excommunication.[126]
- No examples of combined meat and dairy foods can be found in the New Testament.
- The Master was invited into the inner circle of Pharisaic meals.[127] Since this was an exclusive group with strict standards, it suggests that his standards of kosher were reasonably similar to theirs.

## Abraham's Guests

The primary biblical source of opposition to the separation of meat and dairy comes from Genesis 18:8:

Then he took curds and milk and the calf that he had prepared, and set it before them. And he stood by them under the tree while they ate.

In this narrative, Abraham shows hospitality to angelic visitors. Does this suffice as proof of the permissibility of meat and dairy together?

We should note, first of all, that the text does not suggest that the curds and milk were combined with the calf in a single dish. Nor does it say that they ate them both at the same time.

Rather, the Talmudic sages point out the superfluous words "that he had prepared" (literally, "that he made"). Since it is already obvious that the calf was prepared, what additional information is communicated by this phrase? They explain that this indicates that each food was brought when it was ready.[128]

Selecting, slaughtering, and cooking a calf takes considerable time, even when done hastily. If the curds and milk were already prepared, it would make sense not to have his guests wait, but to serve the meal in courses. A long drawn-out meal in courses would be more extravagant and in keeping with the culture. (Even though our translation begins the verse with "then," which implies a strict succession of events, the underlying Hebrew is simply a conversive *vav*, which is normally translated "and," if it is represented in English at all.)

The text is silent about how the meat and dairy were prepared and served; the simplest reading does not by any means suggest it was a single dish. We might speculate that the foods were served together. We might speculate that they were served separately. Both positions are equally speculative, so from a strictly biblical viewpoint, this passage cannot be used as proof of either position.

Even if Genesis 18 were an example of meat and dairy served together, it does not give us license to do so. This narrative is not given in a legislative context. It is a recounting of what actually happened in the real world, not a set of instructions for us to follow. We cannot look at the events in Abraham's life and say, "Since he did it, so can I." That would be a misuse of those stories. After all, the main point in this narrative is the hospitality of Abraham, not his recipes.

Although Abraham obeyed God and kept the Torah to the extent that it was revealed to him, it is not clear what he knew about the commandment in question. Perhaps this instruction would not be made known until the revelation at Sinai.

Genesis also describes how Jacob married two sisters,[129] which is explicitly prohibited by the Torah.[130] And yet Jacob is never criticized by God or anyone for doing so, and even Jewish tradition sees him as extraordinarily righteous. But the fact that Jacob married two sisters does not prove that it is sanctioned by Torah or that we have license to do the same. Nor does it play into how we interpret the Torah's prohibition.

## Significance

The Bible offers absolutely no reason or explanation whatsoever for the commandment not to "boil a young goat in its mother's milk." We are naturally curious as to the significance of this mysterious commandment. However, if our goal is to stay biblical, we must recognize that any explanation for the restriction is human in origin, and it probably falls short of the complete truth. If we mistakenly believe that we know the reason for a commandment, then we will be tempted to break it.

Consider this illustration: A teenage son asks his father if he can take the family car. The father replies, "No," offering no further explanation. The son reasons that he was not given permission to use the car because someone else would need to use it soon. This was a perfectly reasonable inference, which perhaps had even been true in the past. With that in mind, he figures that it should be fine to use it for a quick errand, so he takes it for a spin anyway. But this time, the actual reason his father refused was because the car had faulty brakes that needed immediate repair.

### A Pagan Fertility Ritual?

One common idea is that the prohibition is related to Canaanite ritual practices. If the original prohibition was against a specific idolatrous ritual that involves boiling a baby goat in its mother's milk, one might reason that it should be permitted to combine meat with dairy as long as one does not engage in that pagan practice.

The idea that meat and dairy has connections with idolatry was suggested by Rambam in the twelfth century:

> But as for the prohibition of meat with dairy, while it is undoubtedly a crude and over-filling food, in my opinion it is not a stretch to think that it could be related to idolatry. Perhaps they would eat it during one of their ceremonies or festivals.

> In my opinion, one thing that strengthens this idea of the prohibition of meat with dairy is that the first two times it is mentioned, it is in the context of the pilgrimage festival commandments: "Three times a year," etc. It is as if it is saying, "At your festival, when you come to the house of the Lord your God, do not cook your food there in the particular manner that they used to do." This is more acceptable in my opinion as the reason for the prohibition, although I have not read anything like this in the Sabian books that I have seen.[131]

Thus, Rambam weakly offers this explanation, even though he finds no support for this in his knowledge of pagan ritual. Notably, Rambam does not specifically identify the potential pagan practice as "boiling a young goat in its mother's milk," but just the general idea of "meat with dairy."

In 1929, a Ugaritic[132] text was discovered that appeared to support this theory. A scholar reconstructed one damaged line in the text to say, "Cook a kid in milk, and a lamb in butter."

This seemed at first to confirm scholars' suspicions that the prohibition of meat and dairy was based on idolatrous practices. This reconstructed text quickly permeated scholarship and made its way into many commentaries, such as the *Theological Wordbook of the Old Testament:*

> Since a Ugaritic text (UT 16: Text no. 52:14) specifies, "They cook a kid in milk," the biblical injunction may have been directed against a Canaanite fertility rite.[133]

However, scholars later realized that the reconstruction was inaccurate and corrected it. Nonetheless, this erroneous reading continues to be printed in Bible commentaries. Jack Sasson explains:

> The connection has proven too good to be true. With a better grasp of how Ugaritic poetry works, it is now understood that the string of letters involved contains parts of different phrases, resulting in a passage about pleasing voices that chant about coriander in milk. There's no mention of a goat at all.[134]

Mark S. Smith translates the Ugarit text as "Coriander in milk, Mint in curd," explaining,

> For decades, the phrase *gd bḥlb* was understood as a "kid in milk," based on a brilliant comparison by Ginsberg (1935:65 n. 4 and 72 Postscript) made with Exod 23:19, 34:26, and Deut 14:21. Ginsberg suggested that 1.23 represented a Canaanite ritual practiced presupposed by the biblical prohibitions. The comparison seemed to provide a ritual basis for understanding the biblical injunctions to justify the separation of dairy and meat products: since the "Canaanites" combined such food products as reconstructed for 1.23.14, the Israelites should not do likewise. This interpretation was influential, as it led Gaster (1946:50, 61–62) to situate the text in the springtime rather than in the fall. This view was widely accepted by other scholars as well. However, by the late 1970s, it was becoming clear that 1.23.14 could not sustain this interpretation. No longer could *gd* be a "kid," since in this context "kid" would be spelled *gdy*, as it is in 1.79.4 and 4.150.3 (see also 4.423.23; *DUL* 295). The reading of the line showed a number of other difficulties. In the end, there was no "kid in its milk."[135]

Even if one were to dissent from the scholarly consensus and insist on the "kid in milk, a lamb in butter" interpretation, it still does not justify a hyper-literal and specific reading of the prohibition. The text would not speak of "its *mother's* milk," only "milk."

The inclusion of lamb and butter or curds implies that the supposed pagan practice extended to other combinations of meat and dairy. Nor does it speak of how they are served. Thus, even the faulty reconstruction supports a broad interpretation rather than a narrow one.

An Arabic dish known as *laban ummo*[136] is popular especially in Lebanese cuisine. Sometimes scholars mention this dish in connection with the biblical prohibition, as if perhaps it may have remained from ancient Canaanite ritual until today. The connection is tempting, since *laban ummo* means "its mother's milk" in Arabic. However, numerous facts prevent this from having much significance:

> The earliest reference to the dish is from the tenth century CE, at which time it was called *Madira*. This is still two and a half millennia later than the prohibition in the days of Moses.
>
> *Laban ummo* is not made from goat in milk; it is made from lamb and sometimes beef stewed in yogurt. If this dish had bearing on the question of meat and dairy in Judaism, it would then support a broader interpretation of the animals as well as the dairy in the prohibition.
>
> Even though *laban ummo* literally means "its mother's milk," it is not literally made from the milk of the animal's mother. If the dish had bearing, it would support an idiomatic interpretation of "its mother."
>
> *Laban ummo* has no religious significance. It is a normal, secular dish. If the dish had bearing, it would not support the notion that it was associated with idolatry.

Someone could claim that *laban ummo* evolved over thousands of years from a goat served in its own mother's milk as an idolatrous Canaanite custom and ended up in Lebanese cookbooks as simple meat stewed in yogurt. But that would be pure speculation, since there is no evidence to this effect.

To this date, although claims abound, real evidence of a pagan Canaanite ritual is non-existent.[137]

But suppose Rambam was correct that eating meat with milk was a Canaanite ritual. That only gives us more reason to avoid the combination rather than an excuse to eat it.

## Plenty of Other Explanations

And yet this is not the only reasonable explanation of the prohibition. Others have suggested that it is meant as a sustainable farming practice (not killing the offspring at too young an age), to avoid something that might be perceived as cruel or inhumane, or as a discreet way of speaking against incest.

The most common view in Judaism today is that milk, which sustains the life of a young animal, is a symbol for life. Meat, on the other hand, can only be procured by killing an animal, so it is a symbol of death. If we consider how it is the nature of God to separate things (light from darkness, the waters below from the waters above, the dry land from the seas, each plant and each animal according to its kind, etc.) and the commandments about separation (an ox and a donkey plowing together, two kinds of seed in a field, wool and linen in the same garment, etc.), then perhaps the separation of meat from dairy is along the same lines. But again, this explanation is not made explicit in the biblical text.

# Straining at Gnats

In no uncertain terms, bugs are not biblically kosher (locusts and the like excluded). Western cultures are not accustomed to eating bugs, but many other cultures of the world include different kinds of insects in their diet.

Although we do not typically eat insects knowingly or willingly, bugs make their way into the food we eat. If we do not examine fruits and vegetables carefully, we might very well eat them.

"Straining at gnats" has become a figure of speech for "being overly focused on a minor detail." It comes, of course, from what the Master said:

> Woe to you, scribes and Pharisees, hypocrites! For you
> tithe mint and dill and cumin, and have neglected the
> weightier matters of the law: justice and mercy and faith-

fulness. These you ought to have done, without neglecting the others. You blind guides, straining out a gnat and swallowing a camel! (Matthew 23:23–24)

From the complete context we learn that our Master was not criticizing them for being scrupulous. The fact that they performed minor commandments was not the problem. Rather, their error was their failure to observe the weightier ones. Both gnats and camels are prohibited, or else the Torah would not have said so, and our Master's figure of speech would have no meaning. The correct thing to do is to avoid the camels "without neglecting" straining the gnats. It is not noble to avoid the camels while ignoring the gnats. Remember, our master Yeshua also said,

> Therefore whoever relaxes one of the least of these commandments and teaches others to do the same will be called least in the kingdom of heaven, but whoever does them and teaches them will be called great in the kingdom of heaven. (Matthew 5:19)

It should not be surprising that bugs end up in vegetables. Vegetables grow in the ground. Bugs live in the ground and eat vegetables. But what is surprising is the number of bugs that can be found in vegetables, if you're looking for them, and how sneaky they can be. Sue Fishkoff writes,

> While all vegetables and fruits are inherently kosher, the bugs they attract are not. The Torah warns against consuming insects no less than fifteen times. Jews may not eat an insect that crawls. They may not eat an insect that flies. They may not eat an insect that floats on the water. Chomping down on a piece of curly lettuce that has a bug hiding in its folds could put a Jew in violation of four, five, or more Torah prohibitions, depending on the species and on whether the bug is dead or alive.[138]

Fishkoff explains that changes in food production in recent decades have resulted in a greater amount of bug infestation in produce, leading to heightened awareness among *kashrut* agencies:

The prohibition derives from the Torah, but the strictness with which the law is observed is relatively recent, dating back just a few decades to America's ban on DDT use in agriculture. DDT may present serious health hazards to humans, but it does a bang-up job of killing bugs. The increased popularity of organic produce, which is grown entirely without pesticides, adds further to the infestation problem, rabbis say, making today's fruits and vegetables more bug-ridden, and potentially more unkosher, than ever.[139]

Of course, there has to be a limit on what is prohibited. If every microorganism were off-limits, we couldn't eat anything. Jewish law specifies that bugs are prohibited if they can be seen with the naked eye by the average healthy person. Nonetheless, the difficulty is not in seeing them, but finding them. They hide in cracks and crevasses, blend in with the foliage, and burrow inside the produce. They are often smaller than millimeter in length, and sometimes look like splinters or flecks.

Here are some examples of the most common bugs found in fresh produce:

| Insect | Commonly Found In |
| --- | --- |
| Thrips | artichokes, arugula, asparagus, blackberries, broccoli, cabbage, cauliflower, celery, endives, herbs, lettuce, onions, raspberries, scallions, spinach, strawberries |
| Aphids | artichokes, broccoli, herbs, lettuce, strawberries |
| Worms | arugula, beans, broccoli, Brussels sprouts, cabbage, celery, dates, eggplant, figs, grains, greens (collard, kale, turnip), mushrooms, radishes, rutabaga, spinach, turnips |
| Mites | blackberries, raspberries, strawberries |

Modern *kashrut* agencies have developed a system of checking each type of produce for bugs, not so much as a matter of *halachah* or custom, but from a purely practical perspective. They have learned what types of bugs hide in different food items and how to find and eliminate them. The specific processes of bug-checking are too involved to cover in this document. If you wish to keep biblically kosher, it would be wise to research bug-checking tips from Orthodox Jewish sources. Much information can be found online from reputable organizations such as the Orthodox Union and Star-K.

## Grain, Fruits, and Vegetables

Due to the inherent holiness of the land of Israel, fruits and vegetables grown there are subject to certain prohibitions and laws. The Torah describes several categories of produce which are to be separated from the rest and used for specific purposes.

Some of these laws are not applicable because of the absence of the Temple. Some are partially or completely applicable in the land of Israel. There are also some that have some application outside the land of Israel.

### Bikkurim: The First Fruits

The Torah indicates that the first fruits (*bikkurim*, בִּכּוּרִים) of certain produce grown in the land of Israel must be brought to the Temple and given to a *kohen* (priest) there (Exodus 23:19; Deuteronomy 26:1–11). This refers to the literal first fruits to ripen on the trees, and the sages interpreted the commandment to apply only to the seven species mentioned in Deuteronomy 8:8: wheat, barley, grapes, figs, pomegranates, olives, and dates.

This commandment specifically indicates that the gift is brought to the Temple (Exodus 23:19). Since the Temple does not exist today, this commandment is not in force.[140]

### Trumah Gedolah: The Priestly Contribution

The priestly contribution is called the *trumah gedolah* (תְּרוּמָה גְדוֹלָה, "the great contribution"). This comes from the commandment:

> The firstfruits of your grain, of your wine and of your oil, and the first fleece of your sheep, you shall give him.
> (Deuteronomy 18:4)

In context, "him" refers to the priests (*kohanim*) from the lineage of Aaron. Thus, the first portions of these products have a level of sanctity and may only be eaten by *kohanim*. However, since the commandment refers to the *kohanim* and not the Temple, it is still considered to be in force.

Since the *trumah* has sanctity like the sacrifices, the *kohanim* must be *tahor* (ritually pure) when they eat it. However, in the absence of the Temple, it is impossible for *kohanim* living today to achieve the level of purity necessary to eat *trumah*. On one hand, the portion of *trumah* must be separated from the rest of the produce due to its holiness, but on the other hand, this dedicated portion is unusable. Since it cannot be eaten by the *kohanim*, it must be disposed of properly.

The Torah limits this contribution to grain, grapes, and olives. The sages expanded this requirement to include other types of produce as well. Importantly, they note that the restriction on grain, grapes, and olives is biblical (*de'oraita*), while for other types of produce it is rabbinic (*derabbanan*).[141]

The Torah does not specify what proportion of the produce must be given as *trumah*. The Mishnah records that in the days of the Temple, an average person would give one-fiftieth, or two percent, of their harvest.[142] Since *trumah* is not actually given today, only a miniscule amount is separated and then destroyed.

## Challah: The Contribution of Dough

In addition to the *trumah* of grain, wine, and oil, the Torah describes an additional contribution from dough:

> When you come into the land to which I bring you and when you eat of the bread of the land, you shall present a contribution to the LORD. Of the first of your dough you shall present a loaf as a contribution; like a contribution from the threshing floor, so shall you present it. Some of the first of your dough you shall give to the LORD as a contribution throughout your generations. (Numbers 15:18–21)

The word translated "loaf" is *challah* (חַלָּה). While many people use the term *challah* today to refer to special braided loaves of bread that are eaten on the Sabbath, it technically refers to a small portion of dough that is to be removed from each batch and donated to the priesthood.

Like the *trumah gedolah*, the requirement of giving the *challah* to the priesthood only applies to dough from the land of Israel. Furthermore, it can only be consumed by *kohanim* in a state of ritual purity.

Nonetheless, it is also customary to set aside an olive-sized portion of dough when cooking bread outside of the land of Israel. This Diaspora practice is also recognized as having the force of rabbinic law, not biblical law (that is, it is *derabbanan*, not *de'oraita*).[143]

## Ma'aser Rishon: The Tithe to the Levites

In addition to the priestly contribution (*trumah*), the Torah explains that produce grown in the land of Israel is subject to tithes (*ma'aserot*). Not to be confused with the Christian practice of donating ten percent of one's income to a church,[144] the biblical tithes on produce require farmers to separate portions of their crops for a variety of purposes.

The first tithe that the Torah requires is commonly called the *ma'aser rishon*, or the "first tithe":

> For the tithe of the people of Israel, which they present as a contribution to the LORD, I have given to the Levites for an inheritance. Therefore I have said of them that they shall have no inheritance among the people of Israel. (Numbers 18:24)

This tithe is given not to the *kohanim* (priests) but to the tribe of Levi. However, the tribe of Levi is subsequently required to separate a portion of the *ma'aser rishon* and give it to the *kohanim*. This portion is termed the *trumat ma'aser*, or the "contribution of the tithe":

> Moreover, you shall speak and say to the Levites, "When you take from the people of Israel the tithe that I have given you from them for your inheritance, then you shall present a contribution from it to the LORD, a tithe of the tithe. And your contribution shall be counted to you as though it were the grain of the threshing floor, and as

the fullness of the winepress. So you shall also present a contribution to the LORD from all your tithes, which you receive from the people of Israel. And from it you shall give the LORD's contribution to Aaron the priest. Out of all the gifts to you, you shall present every contribution due to the LORD; from each its best part is to be dedicated." (Numbers 18:26–29)

## Ma'aser Sheni: A Tithe for Celebration

After the first tithe is given, the Torah speaks of an additional tithe requirement:

> You shall tithe all the yield of your seed that comes from the field year by year. And before the LORD your God, in the place that he will choose, to make his name dwell there, you shall eat the tithe of your grain, of your wine, and of your oil, and the firstborn of your herd and flock, that you may learn to fear the LORD your God always. And if the way is too long for you, so that you are not able to carry the tithe, when the LORD your God blesses you, because the place is too far from you, which the LORD your God chooses, to set his name there, then you shall turn it into money and bind up the money in your hand and go to the place that the LORD your God chooses and spend the money for whatever you desire—oxen or sheep or wine or strong drink, whatever your appetite craves. And you shall eat there before the LORD your God and rejoice, you and your household. (Deuteronomy 14:22–26)

This tithe, which is called the *ma'aser sheni* or "second tithe," is not donated to the priesthood or the Levites. Rather, its owners bring it to Jerusalem and eat it in celebration. However, like the *trumah* and the *ma'aser rishon*, the second tithe is sacred and must be eaten in a state of ritual purity. In absence of the Temple, it is customary to redeem the produce dedicated for the *ma'aser sheni* by buying it back with a coin. Then the coin contains the sanctity of the tithe and the produce may be used as normal.

## Ma'aser Ani: A Tithe for the Poor

The Torah speaks of a seven-year agricultural cycle culminating in the sabbatical year, also known as the year of remission (*shmittah*). The *ma'aser sheni* described above only applies during the first, second, fourth, and fifth years of the seven-year sabbatical cycle. On the third and sixth years of the cycle, the tithe is not eaten by the owners. Instead, it is given to the poor:

> And you shall not neglect the Levite who is within your towns, for he has no portion or inheritance with you. At the end of every three years you shall bring out all the tithe of your produce in the same year and lay it up within your towns. And the Levite, because he has no portion or inheritance with you, and the sojourner, the fatherless, and the widow, who are within your towns, shall come and eat and be filled, that the LORD your God may bless you in all the work of your hands that you do. (Deuteronomy 14:27–29)

Further details about this tithe can be found in the passage about the confession of tithes in Deuteronomy 26:12–15.

Judaism does not consider this *ma'aser* to have the same sanctity as the others. This means that it can still be fully observed without the Temple and even in a state of ritual impurity. So today, it is considered a Torah requirement to donate that produce to the poor. Rabbi Reichenberg explains, "One may make an arrangement by which he gives the poor person money instead of the *ma'aser* produce."[145]

Food grown in the land of Israel that has not been tithed as described above has sanctity. A person who eats of sanctified food inappropriately violates the Torah's command:

> But if a priest's daughter is widowed or divorced and has no child and returns to her father's house, as in her youth, she may eat of her father's food; yet no lay person shall eat of it. And if anyone eats of a holy thing unintentionally, he shall add the fifth of its value to it and give the holy thing to the priest. They shall not profane the holy things of the people of Israel, which they contribute to the

LORD, and so cause them to bear iniquity and guilt, by eating their holy things: for I am the LORD who sanctifies them. (Leviticus 22:13–16)

*Kashrut* agencies that oversee food produced in Israel normally ensure that the food is properly tithed. Often, it will indicate on the label, likely in Hebrew. However, if fresh produce is purchased from a market or harvested directly from a garden, it would be important to investigate whether or not it has been tithed.

## Shmittah: The Sabbatical Year

The Torah has special laws regarding produce in the seventh year of the cycle:

> When you come into the land that I give you, the land shall keep a Sabbath to the LORD. For six years you shall sow your field, and for six years you shall prune your vineyard and gather in its fruits, but in the seventh year there shall be a Sabbath of solemn rest for the land, a Sabbath to the LORD. You shall not sow your field or prune your vineyard. You shall not reap what grows of itself in your harvest, or gather the grapes of your undressed vine. It shall be a year of solemn rest for the land. The Sabbath of the land shall provide food for you, for yourself and for your male and female slaves and for your hired servant and the sojourner who lives with you, and for your cattle and for the wild animals that are in your land: all its yield shall be for food. (Leviticus 25:2–7)

> For six years you shall sow your land and gather in its yield, but the seventh year you shall let it rest and lie fallow, that the poor of your people may eat; and what they leave the beasts of the field may eat. You shall do likewise with your vineyard, and with your olive orchard. (Exodus 23:10–11)

This means that there are limits on what kinds of agricultural work may be done during the seventh year. The sages interpreted the statement, "The Sabbath of the land shall provide food for you" (Leviticus 25:6) to imply that produce that grows in the seventh year must be treated with special holiness. Furthermore, because of the ownerless status of the produce, it may not be bought and sold as normal.

In the land of Israel at the time of the seventh year, these commandments can become a practical concern for consumers. *Kashrut* organizations make efforts to ensure that *shmittah* produce is treated properly.

### Orlah: Fruit from the First Years

The Torah regulates how fruit from a tree may be used for the first few years of its growth:

> When you come into the land and plant any kind of tree for food, then you shall regard its fruit as forbidden. Three years it shall be forbidden to you; it must not be eaten. (Leviticus 19:23)

The word for "forbidden" is *orlah*, which elsewhere is the term for "foreskin." Various Jewish scholars have interpreted the term as "blockage" or "surplus matter."

The text of this commandment begins with the clause, "When you come into the land." In most cases, this wording indicates that the commandment only applies in the land of Israel. However, Jewish tradition holds that this is an exception to that pattern.[146] There is some dispute whether the practice of forbidding *orlah* outside the land of Israel bears the weight of a Torah command (*de'oraita*) or is rabbinic (*derabbanan*).[147]

Nonetheless, this law is treated more stringently in the land of Israel. In the land of Israel, fruit may not be eaten if one is uncertain whether it is *orlah* or not. Outside the land of Israel, fruit is only forbidden if it is definitely known to be *orlah*.[148]

The Torah continues with another commandment that gives fruit in the fourth year a special status:

> And in the fourth year all its fruit shall be holy, an offering of praise to the LORD. But in the fifth year you may eat of its fruit, to increase its yield for you: I am the LORD your God. (Leviticus 19:24–25)

Jewish law refers to fourth-year plantings as *neta reva'i* (נֶטַע רְבָעִי), or sometimes just *reva'i*. The phrase translated "holy, an offering of praise" (*kodesh hillulim*, קֹדֶשׁ הִלּוּלִים) has the sense of "something consecrated for praises." According to Jewish interpretation, this sanctity is the same as that of the *ma'aser sheni*,[149] which is also consecrated for praises. That would mean that this type of produce must be brought to Jerusalem and eaten in a state of ritual purity. Just as *ma'aser sheni* cannot be eaten today and so is redeemed, it is customary also to buy back the produce of the fourth year with a coin.

According to some opinions, this law technically applies only to grapevines,[150] but other fruits are included only rabbinically (*derabbanan*). Others accept the face-value reading that it applies to all fruits.

Opinions are split as to whether the sanctity of *reva'i* applies outside the land of Israel, and if so, whether it applies to grapevines or all fruit. Like *orlah*, however, it is only treated as forbidden outside the land when it is definitely known to be unredeemed *reva'i*.

## Kil'ayim: Forbidden Mixtures

The Torah forbids certain types of heterogeneous combinations. These include:

- wearing a combination of wool and linen (called *sha'atnez*)
- allowing differing animal species to mate
- placing two animal species under the same burden
- planting two species of plants in the same place

These prohibited combinations are called *kil'ayim* (כִּלְאָיִם). They are part of a larger theme in the Torah that depicts God as one who creates distinction (*mavdil*, מַבְדִּיל) between things. The creation narrative, for example, largely consists of God making separations and distinctions.

The forbidden mixture most closely related to kosher law is that of combining plants: "You shall not sow your field with two kinds of seed" (Leviticus 19:19). The face-value interpretation of this verse indicates that one must not plant seeds of two different kinds of plants mixed together in the same place. Areas of one's property must thus be exclusively designated for each type of produce.

Since species cannot be planted together, Jewish sages further reasoned that one may not graft two different species of plants or trees together. For example, one may not graft a pomegranate branch onto an orange tree.

This raises some questions regarding other types of combinations. Many types of produce grown today are hybrids, the result of cross-pollination. Although cross-pollination can result in fruit with a combination of genetic material, the Torah does not address or prohibit cross-pollination.

Recent scientific advances have allowed for genetic modification, which can even combine genes of animals with those of plants. This does raise many concerns about *kashrut* as well as ethics. It is beyond the scope of this study to address those issues, although the bottom line is that most authorities[151] do not consider genetic modification to be included in the Torah's prohibition of *kil'ayim*.[152]

*What does this mean for my garden?*

Since the prohibition of mixing seeds is agricultural, Jewish law considers it to be dependent on the land of Israel, with certain exceptions. Outside the land of Israel, Jewish law permits having two different kinds of crops in the same field, such as corn and pumpkins. However, the prohibition of grafting different species of trees is treated far more strictly. Jewish law prohibits it outside of the land of Israel, even for Gentiles according to some opinions. Jewish law also prohibits planting other kinds of produce near a grapevine outside of the land.[153]

However, while the Torah prohibits planting different kinds of seeds together, it does not prohibit *using* or *eating* the resulting fruit. That simple fact eliminates most of the *kashrut* concerns.

## Portions for the Poor

The Torah instructs that certain portions of the field are to be given to the poor. This includes the corners of the field, gleanings, scattered and fallen grapes in the vineyard, and forgotten sheaves

(Leviticus 19:10, 23:22; Deuteronomy 24:19–21). This law is also considered to apply only in the land of Israel.

Is this a *kashrut* concern? One might consider this similar to the issues of *trumah* and *ma'aser*. If someone does not observe these commandments and the designated portions are intermingled with the bulk of the produce, then would that make the entire crop off-limits?

Since the gifts for the poor do not have Temple sanctity like *trumah* and *ma'aser*, it is not an issue of defilement of holy things or *kashrut*. Yet, if a person inappropriately eats of these designated portions, they could be considered stealing.

However, if no poor people are gleaning from fields, a field owner can use that produce. The Torah does not require him to leave it to rot or have it eaten by animals. For this reason, the portions for the poor are not considered to be a problem in Israeli produce today.

## Food Offered to Idols

One of the apostolic injunctions for Gentiles is to "abstain from what has been sacrificed to idols" (Acts 15:20, 15:29, 21:25). This requirement is not only for Gentiles. In Jewish practice, this prohibition comes from the Torah:

> Take care, lest you make a covenant with the inhabitants of the land to which you go, lest it become a snare in your midst ... lest you make a covenant with the inhabitants of the land, and when they whore after their gods and sacrifice to their gods and you are invited, you eat of his sacrifice. (Exodus 34:12, 15)

### The Basics

In Jewish law, the prohibition of idolatry focuses most directly on wine. Although it can easily be derived from the passage in Exodus quoted above, the Torah's ban on drinking idolatrous wine offerings is also implicit in Deuteronomy 32:38.

Jewish law treats prohibition of idolatrous food and wine very stringently. Whereas inadvertent contamination by non-kosher substances in tiny amounts can be overlooked, even the slightest amount of a substance associated with idolatry is banned. One is not even permitted to benefit from it in any way. This is based on the laws of the idolatrous city in Deuteronomy 13:13–19[12–18]. In this passage we read, "None of the devoted things shall stick to your hand" (Deuteronomy 13:18[17]); that is to say, do not keep any amount of the forbidden items in that city. Furthermore, the Torah commands,

> And you shall not bring an abominable thing into your house and become devoted to destruction like it. You shall utterly detest and abhor it, for it is devoted to destruction. (Deuteronomy 7:26)

In modern society, it is not common to use food in idolatrous rituals, especially not food that will be sold to the public. Occasionally, a Chinese or Indian restaurant may have a statue or shrine, even in a restaurant that has kosher certification. This could understandably make a person squeamish. While it is not an acceptable practice, it may not be an issue that disqualifies the food if the statue is merely for decorative purposes.

## What about Halal?

*Halal* (حلال) is an Arabic term meaning "legally permitted," and it is often used to describe food that may be eaten according to Muslim law. In the Islamic religion, there are parameters for permitted and forbidden foods just as there are laws of *kashrut* in Judaism.

In Islam it is customary to pronounce the name of Allah over food that is to be eaten in a formal invocation called the *basmala* (بسملة). It is also customary to pronounce the *basmala* when slaughtering an animal.[154]

Does this ritual of invocation cause *halal* food or meat to be considered "offered to idols"? Regarding meat, this question is somewhat moot. Islamic standards of ritual slaughter do not rise to the level of kosher and would not be allowed by Jewish law. Even for Gentiles, it seems doubtful that *halal* meat would rise to the standard set by Acts 15.

Setting this aside, there are some questions that must be answered to determine whether *halal* meat is considered an idol offering. First, although there is no question that Islam is not an acceptable or correct belief system, being incorrect or even heretical is not necessarily the same as being idolatrous. Does Islam rise to the level of idolatry?

The name Allah is simply the Arabic word meaning "God," a contraction of *al-ilah* ("the god"). It is cognate with the Hebrew words for God *el* (אֵל), *eloah* (אֱלוֹהַ), and *elohim* (אֱלֹהִים), the Aramaic words *elah* (אֱלָה) and *elaha* (אֱלָהָא), and the Syriac *alaha* (ܐܠܗܐ). Arabic-speaking Christians used the name Allah for God prior to the existence of Islam.[155]

Muslims view Allah as the one and only God who created all things, and they identify Allah as the same God worshiped by Jews and Christians. Despite the tension that has often existed between the Jewish and Islamic communities, Jewish law does not classify Islam as idolatrous. Furthermore, when an animal is slaughtered in accordance with Islamic custom, the *basmala* is spoken, but the animal is not placed on an altar or burned as an offering. Thus, from the perspective of Jewish law, *halal* meat would not be considered as sacrificed to idols, although it would not be considered kosher.

Since *halal* simply means that something is permitted for Muslims, foods other than meat may also be considered *halal*. Today, there are agencies that certify that foods contain only what is permitted for Muslims, just as there are *kashrut* supervision organizations in Judaism. If a Muslim organization places their stamp of approval on a product, it does not have any effect on its kosher status for Jews.

A clause in the Quran[156] also permits Muslims to eat the meat of the "people of the book," a term referring to Jews and Christians. Thus, some Muslims accept kosher-slaughtered meat as *halal*.

### Why isn't halal considered kosher?

Considering the fact that Muslims slaughter animals without stunning and drain the blood, one might wonder why *halal* slaughter does not qualify as kosher. There are numerous reasons, including these:

| Kosher | Halal | Additional Notes |
|---|---|---|
| Camels, rabbits, and shellfish may not be eaten | Camels, rabbits, and shellfish may be eaten. | Cross-contamination is a possibility. |
| Meat may not be removed until the animal is technically dead. | Meat might be removed before the animal is dead from the perspective of Jewish law. | This would be considered eating the limb of a live animal, which is prohibited even for Noachides. |
| Wounded animals may not be slaughtered. | Wounded animals, such as those that are hunted, may be slaughtered. | |
| The windpipe must not be cut during slaughter, so that the animal does not choke or die of asphyxiation. | The windpipe must be completely cut during slaughter. | This would render the animal "strangled" according to Jewish law and prohibited by Acts 15. |
| The sciatic nerve (*gid hanasheh*) may not be eaten and is removed during slaughter. | The *gid hanasheh* may be eaten and is not removed. | |
| Certain fat portions (*chelev*) may not be eaten and are removed during slaughter. | *Chelev* may be eaten and is not removed. | |
| Meat must be kept separate from dairy. | Meat does not need to stay separate from dairy. | |
| Meat must be soaked and salted to remove as much residual blood as possible. | Meat does not need to be soaked and salted. | |

| Kosher | Halal | Additional Notes |
| --- | --- | --- |
| The slaughter must be performed in one uninterrupted stroke. If this not done, the meat is not kosher. | The slaughter should be performed in one uninterrupted stroke, but if it is not, it is still *halal*. | This would also render the animal "strangled" and prohibited by Acts 15. |
| Due to the amount of detail and skill required with kosher slaughter, Judaism only allows observant Jewish individuals with rigorous training to perform slaughter. | Islam merely requires that the person who performs the slaughter be a man, woman, or child of sound mind who is a Muslim, or by some standards, a Jew or Christian. | |

## Hidden Ingredients

In today's world, food production has become extremely complex. Just one century ago, it would have been likely that most of the ingredients in the food you ate would have been produced by people you knew personally. Today, in one packaged product, dozens of ingredients appear that might have originated literally across the planet. In order for foods to endure packaging, shipping, and storage, chemicals and additives have to be added to the food such as emulsifiers and preservatives. Factories add colors and flavors to the food to increase its taste and visual appeal. Some additives are used to streamline the production process or decrease costs. To some extent, the U.S. government requires that ingredients be listed, but in many cases, ingredients may be omitted from the list. Others are hidden behind vaguely worded ingredient names or general categories such as "natural flavors."

The list of problematic ingredients in food is incredibly long and cannot be reproduced here, but here is a sample of a few issues:

- **Carmine** (also called cochineal) is a red food color derived from insects, found in many items, including fruit juices, baked goods, spices, and meat.

- **Gelatin**, a well-known gelling agent, comes from animal hides, bones, or hooves, and is found in items such as yogurt, marshmallows, jams, margarine, and ice cream.
- **Anti-caking agents** are often made from animal fats, and they are found in spice powders and blends.
- **Glycerides** are often made from animal fats, and they are found in sauces, dressings, and ice creams.
- Many **natural flavorings** are derived from animal products such as extracts from beaver, cat, or deer glands.

Aside from ingredients in the food, in many cases it is necessary to use *food-grade oils* for lubrication of machinery in food-processing plants. Food-grade oil is necessary specifically because the oils may come in contact with the food. Many of these food-grade oils come from animals. For example, sperm [whale] oil is used on bakery pans.[157]

The world of food production has changed dramatically. It is now impossible to keep a biblical kosher standard simply by reading labels. There are simply too many factors involved in food production.

## Cheese

Cheese is another great example of a product that would seem perfectly kosher, but could very well pose a problem. Of course, added flavors, colors, anti-caking agents, preservatives, and additives that modify the texture of the cheese raise concerns. However, an essential ingredient in cheese is the complex of enzymes known as rennet, which is added in order to coagulate the milk. Rennet is traditionally derived from the stomach lining of calves, but pig enzymes can also be used.

> Owing to the increasing world production of cheese (roughly 2–3% per annum over the past 30 years) and the reduced supply of calf vells (due to a decrease in calf

numbers and a tendency to slaughter calves at an older age), the supply of calf rennet has been inadequate for many years. This has led to an increase in the price of veal rennet and to a search for rennet substitutes. Despite the availability of numerous potentially useful milk coagulants, only six rennet substitutes (all aspartyl proteinases) have been found to be more or less acceptable for cheese production: bovine, porcine, and chicken pepsins and the acid proteinases from *Rhizomucor miehei, R. pusillus,* and *Chryphonectria parasitica.*[158]

Fortunately, porcine (that is, pig) pepsin is becoming less common. Instead more cheese producers use microbial sources for the rennet, which could alleviate some *kashrut* concerns.

Jewish law does not consider animal rennet in milk to be a forbidden combination of meat and dairy. However, since the rennet comes from an animal's stomach, the animal must be a kosher species. Furthermore, it must be slaughtered in a kosher manner. This requirement would disqualify any cheese containing animal rennet from a source that is not specifically kosher. If the cheese producer uses exclusively microbial rennet, these concerns would be also be alleviated.

Beyond these biblical concerns, there is an additional overarching safeguard required by rabbinic law: Cheese produced by non-Jews is forbidden.[159] The specific reason for this is not explained in the Mishnah, but the Gemara[160] posits some theories, including health issues, contamination from non-kosher food, and association with idolatry. This requires that an observant Jew be present at the facility to supervise and possibly to activate some of the equipment. Consequently, this also limits the ability of the plant to operate on the Sabbath.

Some *kashrut* agencies (such as the Orthodox Union) feel that this prohibition only applies to solid cheeses that are coagulated with rennet (microbial or otherwise), but soft cheeses that are coagulated with acid are acceptable without direct Jewish involvement. This is why cream cheese, cottage cheese, and some kinds of mozzarella are often certified kosher without a substantially higher price.

# Kosher Certification

The best way, then, to ensure that the food that one eats is kosher is to purchase only products that have a certifying mark from a kosher supervision agency. These symbols are ubiquitous, and can be found on just about any type of food that can possibly be kosher.

A kosher certification symbol is called a *hechsher*. Hechshers are symbols that represent agencies that conduct kosher supervision. A *mashgiach* is an expert trained in kosher law who inspects and supervises food production to ensure that it meets the proper standards. He will check all ingredients and processes to make sure that the food qualifies. If it does, the manufacturer will be allowed to place a hechsher on the product label. It is unlawful to place a hechsher on a label without approval, since it is a trademarked logo owned by the particular certifying agency.

Each agency might have its own standards and leniencies. For this reason, it is important to choose only reliable, recognized hechshers.

Years ago, a simple letter K was often used to indicate that an item was kosher. However, a plain K cannot be trademarked, so there is nothing to prevent manufacturers from using it on their labels without any approval whatsoever. Therefore, today, a plain K no longer can be trusted as a kosher symbol.

The two most well known and respected kosher symbols are Ⓚ and Ⓤ. However, there are numerous other hechshers that are equally reliable. The hechshers available vary regionally.

## "Leaven" on Passover

On Passover, we are given an additional kosher law:

> Seven days you shall eat unleavened bread [*matzah*]. On the first day you shall remove leaven [*se'or*] out of your houses, for if anyone eats what is leavened [*chametz*], from the first day until the seventh day, that person shall be cut off from Israel. (Exodus 12:15)

There are three key terms in this verse. *Matzah* (מַצָּה) is typically translated "unleavened bread." *Se'or* (שְׂאֹר) is typically translated "leaven." *Chametz* (חָמֵץ) is typically translated "what is leavened" or "leavened bread."

However, these translations can be misleading. The Hebrew terms do not refer to "leaven" or "leavening" in the sense that we use the word today. In ancient times, as well as in breads such as sourdough today, bread could be leavened just by allowing the dough to sit for a period of time until biochemical processes begin.

*Chametz* thus refers to products made of certain kinds of grain that have come in contact with water and are allowed to sit for a period of time without being cooked.

Most scholars see the word *chametz* as being related to a root meaning "to become sour; to ferment." Other terms related to this root are *chometz* (חוֹמֶץ), "vinegar," and *chamutz* (חָמוּץ), "sour." Alternatively, some scholars connect the term with *chamas* (חָמָס), which literally means "violence."[161]

Keep in mind that the Hebrew word *chametz* does not imply anything about the fluffiness or softness of the food. This is one area where our English language leads us astray. *Chametz* can take many forms: not just fluffy bread, but also even noodles, cookies, or drinks.

*Se'or* refers to an inedible lump of starter dough that contains a high concentration of yeast. *Se'or* is used to expedite the fermentation process in a new batch of dough. However, yeast itself is not *chametz* or *se'or*. By itself, it is a unicellular fungus that is very common in the environment, and it can be used both in foods that are *chametz* and those that are not.

*Matzah* is flat bread that is made with flour and water and baked quickly at a high temperature. This ends the biochemical processes that would otherwise make it *chametz*.

### The Five Grains

*Chametz* is limited to grain products, which is borne out by the fact that wine and wine vinegar are present and consumed during Passover in the Gospels. This makes sense, because it was bread making at the time of the exodus that led to the prohibition of *chametz*. Bread, as it was known to the ancient Israelites, could be made of five types of grain.

The Hebrew terms for the five grains[162] are:

- *chittim* (חיטים), biblically *chittah* (חיטה): commonly translated "wheat"
- *se'orim* (שעורים): commonly translated "barley"
- *kusmin* (כוסמין), biblically *kussemet* (כסמת): commonly translated "emmer" or "spelt"
- *shibbolet shu'al* (or *shi'al*) (שיבולת שועל): commonly translated "oats"
- *shifon* (or *shippon*) (שיפון): commonly translated "rye"

There are multiple opinions as to the exact identity of some of these grains. Gil Marks offers this explanation:

> The Five Species are *chittim*, *se'orim*, *kusmin*, *shippon*, and *shibbolet shi'al*, which probably refer, respectively, to naked wheat varieties (the husks are loosely attached to the seed), including durum and bread wheat, six-rowed barley, emmer, einkorn, and two-rowed barley.[163]

While the tradition to avoid oats and rye is strong in Jewish practice and dates back at least about a thousand years, these plants were probably not cultivated in Israel at the time of the Bible or the Mishnah. As Professor Yehudah Felix points out,[164] the Mishnah considers *shibbolet shu'al* and *se'orim* as one species, allowing them both to be planted in the same field without violating Leviticus 19:19 and Deuteronomy 22:9.[165] But oats and barley are not similar or closely related, which suggests that they are not the proper identification of those species.

Since other products that we conventionally think of as grain (such as rice or corn) would not have been cultivated by ancient Israelites, they do not constitute *chametz*.

One might ask: Is it really reasonable to limit *chametz* to those five grains? After all, there are other biologically-similar cereal grains in which fermentation can also occur, such as corn (maize) or rice. Ashkenazi custom places those grains, along with legumes and certain other foods, in a different category called *kitniyos*. Certain Jewish communities choose to avoid *kitniyos* in addition to *chametz* because they could be easily confused, but not because of an explicit commandment in the Torah. But is that classification correct, or should maize and rice be prohibited as a matter of Torah law?

One commonality shared by these five species is their high amount of gluten. Gluten traps carbon dioxide released during fermentation. This is why gluten-free bread or bread made from rice or corn is so different from fluffy, soft loaves of wheat bread.

While maize and rice are biologically similar to the five grains, biological taxonomy is markedly different from biblical taxonomy, as we have seen elsewhere in our kosher study. For example, the Bible classifies bats along with birds and whales along with fish. That is because the major biblical taxonomic classification is the domain in which the creature lives: those that teem in the water, those that crawl on the earth, beasts of the field, and birds of the air. It is reasonable to apply this also to plants. This suggests that a biological classification may not be useful from a biblical perspective; a classification based on native land is more in keeping with biblical thought.

For example, compare Egypt's choice foods: "the cucumbers, the melons, the leeks, the onions, and the garlic" (Numbers 11:5) with those of Israel: "a land of wheat and barley, of [grape] vines and fig trees and pomegranates, a land of olive trees and [date] honey" (Deuteronomy 8:8). Notice how those of Egypt all grow directly on the ground (downwards), whereas those of Israel, aside from grain, all grow in trees (upwards).

(One might mention that grapes don't grow on trees; they grow on vines. But there is another example of Biblical taxonomy at odds with biological taxonomy: Biblically, a grape vine is a tree, as we can see from verses such as Judges 9:12, Ezekiel 15:2–6, and others.)

The sages considered wheat and barley to be the primary grain species and the other three to be subspecies. This would explain why the Scriptures so frequently mention wheat and barley but so rarely mention the other three in any context, despite the fact that they did exist and were in use at the time.

Nonetheless, look at how many different terms for grain are used in the Torah, specifically in connection with Egypt:

> The flax and the **barley** [se'orah] were struck down, for
> the barley was in the ear and the flax was in bud. But the

**wheat** [*chittah*] and the **emmer** [*kussemet*] were not struck down, for they are late in coming up. (Exodus 9:31–32)

And he fell asleep and dreamed a second time. And behold, seven ears of **grain** [*shibbolim*, plural of *shibbolet*], plump and good, were growing on one stalk. (Genesis 41:5)

## Becoming Chametz

The Hebrew term for the process of becoming *chametz* is *chimmutz* (חִימוּץ). But what exactly is this process in chemical terms?

There are two major biochemical processes involved in making bread when flour or grain comes in contact with water:

> First, enzymes present in the grain break down the complex starches into more simple sugars. This process is called starch degradation.

> Then, yeast (which occurs naturally in the environment) begins to transform the sugars into alcohol, releasing carbon dioxide gas. This process is called fermentation. (In bread, the carbon dioxide released in fermentation is trapped by strands of gluten in the dough, resulting in a fluffy texture.)

It is unlikely that people in pre-modern times perceived or understood the distinction between starch degradation and fermentation. However, they were keen observers and noted ways that these processes could be enhanced or suppressed.

Since starch degradation is a prerequisite to yeast fermentation, it can be seen as a first step in the fermentation process. However, yeast does not need to be present for starch degradation to occur. So while fermentation is certainly in view in the ancient conception of *chimmutz*, it can begin immediately even without yeast.

It is impossible to have bread in which absolutely no *chimmutz* has occurred. The biochemical processes of *chimmutz* end when the product is cooked, since heat deactivates yeast and denatures enzymes. Thus, for bread to be "unleavened," there has to be a defined maximum amount of time between when the flour comes in contact with water and when baking is completed. The Bible does not tell us what that time is.

Jewish law defines *chametz* as any of the above-listed grain products that has been combined with water and has been allowed to sit longer than eighteen minutes before being cooked.[166]

While it sounds like an arbitrary number, eighteen minutes is a basic unit of time in Jewish law. Prior to more accurate and accessible timekeeping methods, durations were often estimated based on the amount of time it takes to perform simple tasks such as uttering a particular phrase, eating a loaf of bread, or walking a certain distance. Eighteen minutes is the estimated time that it takes to walk the length of a *mil* (about two-thirds of a modern mile or about one kilometer).

## Examples of Chametz

This means that many foods you might not expect can be considered *chametz*, such as noodles, crackers, or cookies as well as both fluffy loaves of bread and flatbreads such as pitas or tortillas. Ultimately, that means any grain product in your house other than kosher-for-Passover matzah.

Other types of microbiological processes are not prohibited, so foods with bacterial cultures such as yogurt or natural sauerkraut can be kept as long as they do not contain other problematic ingredients. Fermentation itself is only prohibited for the five grains listed above, but other kinds of fermentation are allowed. Rabbi Eliyahu Kitov relates an interesting custom based on this fact:

> It was customary in many Jewish communities—and the practice is still widespread—for people to pickle beets and other vegetables before Pesach for use during the Festival … The Torah says that any food which has fermented may not be eaten on Pesach. The Sages explained that the laws of *chametz* apply only to grains. The Sadducees, who denied the authenticity of the orally transmitted Torah, explained the verse literally and expanded the prohibition to include any food that had fermented. Although their interpretation was more strict than that of our Sages, their stringency was a denial of the oral tradition. Therefore, it

became customary to make a point of eating these pickled foods on Pesach in order to demonstrate that we reject the interpretation of the Sadducees and follow only the teachings of our Sages.[167]

Other leavening agents (such as baking soda) that release gases through a non-biological process are not prohibited either. So you wouldn't need to remove a canister of baking soda, although you probably should not use it during Passover in a way that would involve combining flour with water.

Grain vinegar is a fermented grain product, and so it is forbidden. Grain vinegar is present in many foods, such as ketchup and mustard. If the label does not indicate what type of vinegar it is, it is quite likely from grain. Other vinegars such as from cider or wine are not prohibited, as long as they are not combined with grain vinegar as well.

Many alcohols are also produced from fermenting grain. Beer and many spirits are thus prohibited. Alcohols that are not made from grain are not prohibited, such as wine from grapes. Grain alcohol is present in many food flavorings, such as vanilla extract. It is likely present in trace amounts in any food that lists "natural flavors" on the label.

Most people remove flour before Passover as well. If it is perfectly dry, flour is not *chametz*, but if by accident or negligence your flour comes in contact with moisture it will become *chametz*. Removing flour also removes that possibility.

The safest way to know if something is kosher for Passover is if a reliable "kosher for Passover" certification appears on the label. Often, this appears as a letter P alongside the standard hechsher.

## Conclusion

As you can see, there is much more to learn from the Bible about kosher law than pure and impure species. Commercial meats from pure species contain forbidden parts of the animal as well as blood, and may not have been killed in accordance with biblical standards. Animal products can crop up in the most unexpected places. Biblical sources point to cleansing dishes through a heating process. "You shall not boil a young goat in its mother's milk" is a deceptively narrow translation, and a simple linguistic examination can suggest a separation of meat and dairy. Thorough insect-checking of fruits and vegetables is an important part of kosher food preparation. On Passover, we must abstain not just from fluffy bread, but from most grain foods aside from matzah, including many foods that contain vinegar or flavorings.

Hopefully, this book has awakened you to more of the issues involved in keeping a biblical standard of kosher. Much more could be said about biblical kosher law. Perhaps this study has helped contribute to your sense of respect for the definitions and interpretations that have arisen from the Jewish community as they have found ways to keep the biblical law over thousands of years.

Between hidden ingredients, complex food production methods, mistranslations, and varying interpretations and standards, keeping kosher has the potential of being confusing and exhausting. People who want to take on a fully biblical standard of eating will find it easier to adopt and rely on conventional standards of *kashrut* rather than trying to make their own way. This makes sense, because the Torah is not meant to be observed in a vacuum. It was not given to individuals, but to a nation, and the entire nation is intended to uphold it together.

Biblical kosher practice does not have to be all or nothing. One can begin with a single step and move into more observance gradually. Every step counts. And yet, it is important to have a sense of the big picture and an understanding that keeping biblical kosher is more than the avoidance of pork and shellfish.

For individuals who are interested in becoming more observant of kosher law, these books may prove very useful:

- Rabbi Binyomin Forst, *The Kosher Kitchen: A Practical Guide* (Brooklyn: Mesorah Publications, 2009).
  This book is very thorough and detailed. It provides guidance from an Orthodox perspective, explaining both Ashkenazi and Sephardi customs. It is organized by topic and is good for reference, also providing practical examples. It explains how to make dishes, surfaces, and appliances kosher,

how to operate in a kosher kitchen, and how to solve problems that may arise.

- Lisë Stern, *How to Keep Kosher: A Comprehensive Guide to Understanding Jewish Dietary Laws* (New York: HarperCollins, 2004).
This book describes different approaches to *kashrut* (Reform, Conservative, and Orthodox) in general terms. It focuses on how to transition from a non-kosher to kosher kitchen. It provides special instructions for the Sabbath and Passover and includes recipes.

- Zalman Goldstein, *Going Kosher in 30 Days* (Jewish Learning Group, Inc., 2007).
This book is written from a Chabad (Chasidic) perspective. Rather than by topic, the information in this book is arranged chronologically, with basic, important topics first and details later.

- Rabbi Binyomin Forst, *The Laws of Kashrus* (Brooklyn: Mesorah Publications, 1999).
This book is not for the beginner. For someone with a basic understanding of kosher law, it provides technical details. It is good as a reference book.

# PART 3

# KEEPING KOSHER IN A MESSIANIC COMMUNITY

By Aaron Eby and Toby Janicki

B ecause of the centrality of food to human sociology, physiology, and psychology, it unfortunately has the potential to bring out the worst in us. *Kashrut* can thus become one of the biggest challenges a Messianic community faces.

## Kashrut and Community

When one person is not willing to eat another person's food, it is natural for the one who offered it to feel offended and take it personally. There is a tendency to feel that it is the person himself, rather than the food, that is being rejected. To him, the rejection implies that he is on a lower spiritual plane. He feels like he is considered unclean and not good enough. It is as though he was called ignorant or untrustworthy. The rejected person may suppose that the person who declined it has a judgmental attitude.

With this in mind, one must handle this kind of situation with delicacy and tact. The person upholding a standard of *kashrut* can do a few things to minimize the offense:

One step you can take is to keep your kosher standard consistent. It may need to change and grow over time, but you should have clearly defined reasons for each practice you observe. This helps to show that it is not a personal issue, but is specifically about the food.

Second, communicate your needs up front. It is far more disappointing for people to have their food rejected after they have already spent time and money preparing it.

A third guideline is to make every effort to learn what you *can* eat. Learning what is permissible is just as much a part of Torah as learning what is forbidden. Often, people who are less knowledgeable about *kashrut* can be overly strict in their observance because they want to err on the safe side. In circumstances where strictly kosher food is not available, there are certain exceptions that people can make, even according to Orthodox Judaism. One should not violate his convictions, but it is wise to learn which practices are mere safeguards that may be lifted in some circumstances. Along these lines, it is better to find ways to help people show you hospitality and generosity than to reject their invitation outright.

Finally, the stricter a person's observance is, the more important it is to put effort into showing sincere grace, compassion, and kindness to others. This can help counteract the automatic perception that a kosher-keeper is judgmental or unloving.

Another type of offense can happen when a person is perceived as being too "rabbinic." One may reason that if people take on practices that they believe to be non-biblical and therefore non-obligatory, they may make it too difficult to eat together with others. In their minds, such a person would be sacrificing the biblical value of "table fellowship" at the altar of conformity to Orthodox Judaism.

However, as this study has shown, many traditional aspects of keeping kosher have more biblical support than people realize.

Furthermore, while choices to keep kosher may present some challenges and new situations, they would not have to be a barrier to "table fellowship." Fellowship is about people, not food. Each party should make reasonable accommodations for the other, just as one would do so for a person with diabetes or allergies or who is vegan. The instruction to "eat what is set before you" (1 Corinthians 10: 27) is in the context of questions of idolatry, not *kashrut*. Furthermore, it places the onus upon the guest, not the host; it does not by any means imply that one may serve less-than-kosher food to a guest who requires it. Fellowship does not have to be complicated, nor does it require a gourmet meal.

There are a few steps that communities can take that may help prevent *kashrut* from becoming a source of conflict:

One important step is to cultivate an atmosphere of diversity of practice and mutual acceptance. *Kashrut* is a complicated issue, and not everyone will see things the same way. Furthermore, people need time to transition and space to grow in their observance. Communities must encourage members to give people latitude to have different personal standards, whether they are stricter or more lenient on a particular matter. Community leaders would do well to teach people not to be offended when others won't eat their food.

## Community Kashrut Standard

Meals are a common component of Messianic communities, and often members are encouraged to bring dishes to share. As a result, congregations find it necessary to establish a community standard of *kashrut*. This standard need not (and probably should not) define people's observance in their own homes, but it provides a frame of reference for what people can expect at a congregational event.

When setting a standard for the community to observe, there are a few points to consider. First, no matter how high you set the standard, there will always be someone who still can't eat it. Second, no matter how low you set the standard, someone will bring food that does not meet it.

In general, it is best to shoot for the highest standard that can practically be achieved for community functions, for a number of reasons: It will it allow the greatest number of people to eat without compromise. Also, it will be difficult to raise the standard later on after people establish patterns and habits. It also would reflect poorly on our Master Yeshua for a Messianic Jewish congregation to be serving non-kosher food.

In a Messianic congregation where people contribute foods that they prepared at home, it will be practically impossible to achieve a fully traditional kosher standard. Orthodox synagogues do not generally provide meals potluck-style. Rather, people contribute money, and the food is purchased and provided by a member of the synagogue staff. For example, someone may sponsor a meal in honor of someone's birthday or anniversary.

A Messianic congregation would probably need to adopt the sponsorship model if they wish to have complete control over the kosher status of the food. But if this is not practical in a particular case, it should still be possible to accommodate people on the stricter end of observance by providing pre-packaged foods that have a reliable hechsher and being careful about how they are opened and served.

## Kashrut for Gentiles

So far, we have examined what it means to keep biblically kosher in everyday life. The information we have presented arises from the view that the complete spectrum of the Torah's dietary laws are incumbent upon Jewish people today. Now let's examine the biblical perspective regarding the dietary requirements of people who are not Jewish.

### Vegetarian Beginnings

Immediately after creating man and woman, God instructed them about what may and may not be eaten. This suggests that that the general concept of dietary laws is universal in scope. Although it is not enumerated among the traditional 613 commandments of the Torah, one of God's first instructions to mankind explained what he may eat:

> And God said, "Behold, I have given you every plant yield-ing seed that is on the face of all the earth, and every tree with seed in its fruit. You shall have them for food. And to every beast of the earth and to every bird of the heavens and to everything that creeps on the earth, everything that has the breath of life, I have given every green plant for food." And it was so. (Genesis 1:29–30)

Humanity's first diet was vegetarian, and it would remain this way until after the flood.[168] This implies that God's instruction to subdue the earth and dominate the animals (Genesis 1:28) has limits. Humans must receive divine permission regarding what they may or may not eat.

Why did God decree a vegetarian diet for Adam? According to one explanation, it was in order "that man should be humbled by withholding his authority to kill other animals."[169] Rav Kook views the human consumption of meat as a result of our fallen state and further postulates that, based on prophetic passages such as Isaiah 11:7 and 65:25, in the Messianic Age the world will return to vegetarianism.[170] (Prophecies about the resumption of the sacrificial system, however, contradict this idea. Several sacrifices require the consumption of sacrificial cuts of meat.)

A vegetarian diet eliminates many dietary issues, and for Gentiles, it may be one of the easiest ways to keep biblically kosher. The early Jewish sect of believers in Yeshua called the Ebionites also adopted a vegetarian diet. According to church tradition, some of the apostles practiced a form of vegetarianism.[171]

## Eating is Spiritual

While eating is one of the most basic and primal of human instincts, it should not be taken for granted. Through controlling one's appetites, a person can rise above his animalistic nature.

Eating is an inherently spiritual act, and this is true for both Jews and Gentiles. For example, eating provides fuel to the body and enables people to carry out their service of God. Rabbi Eliyahu ben Moshe Vidash wrote that "our eating for this elevated purpose—for the sake of Heaven—can bring us to holiness and cleaving to God."[172]

Consequently, eating has the potential to be a spiritually uplifting activity, but if it is abused, it can also have negative spiritual effects. Just as God's first instructions to mankind involved food, so did man's first sin. Although man was instructed not to eat of the tree of the knowledge of good and evil,[173] it would not be long before he transgressed:

> So when the woman saw that the tree was good for food, and that it was a delight to the eyes, and that the tree was to be desired to make one wise, she took of its fruit and ate, and she also gave some to her husband who was with her, and he ate. Then the eyes of both were opened, and they knew that they were naked. And they sewed fig leaves together and made themselves loincloths. (Genesis 3:6–7)

Even before the time of Moses, a person's failure to control his appetite often led to his spiritual downfall, such as Esau's foolish sale of his birthright.[174] The same theme occurs in Jacob's deception of Isaac in Genesis 27, which begins with Isaac's craving for Esau's savory game. Even the Israelites in the wilderness incite God's anger as they fall prey to their animal cravings and complain for having no meat, despite the miraculous provision of the manna.[175] Additionally, the Torah specifically warns Israel not to become arrogant and forget God once they "eat and are satisfied" (Deuteronomy 8:11–14). Yaakov Levinson comments that according to some rabbinic sources, all sins are related to food:

> In *Tanna D'vay Eliyahu*, the prophet Elijah is claimed to acrimoniously blame all our troubles on eating: "I call Heaven and Earth to bear witness that all the children of man are gathered to death and all creatures descend to sorrow only because of eating and drinking" (*Eliyahu Zuta* 3). The commentary *Zikukin D'Nura* explains that all sins result from overindulging in food and drink.[176]

### Noah and Kosher

We do not encounter the concept of pure and impure animals until the time of Noah. God instructs Noah to take with him "seven pairs of all clean animals" and only one "pair of the animals that are not clean."[177] The term translated "clean" here is *tahor*, the term that Leviticus 11 and Deuteronomy 14 use to describe intrinsically pure species of animals that Israel may eat. However, rather than using the typical word *tamei* ("impure") to describe the other animals, the passage uses the phrase *lo tahor*, which literally means "not pure." Rashi explains that in this passage *tahor* means, "that which is destined to be pure for Israel"—in other words, animals permitted in Leviticus 11 and Deuteronomy 14.[178] Thus it would not be fitting to describe the other animals as *tamei*, because they are *tamei* only for Israel, which did not exist at that point in time. By using *lo tahor*, God indicates that although these animals are permissible as food to other nations, they will not be permissible to Israel and are therefore ineligible for sacrifice. Remarkably, this passage implies that the designations of "pure" and "impure" must have been taught orally long before they were given to the Jewish people in Leviticus and Deuteronomy.

Since Noah did not eat meat before the flood, the categories "pure" and "impure" only related to sacrifice rather than food. Accordingly, Genesis 8:20 explains that Noah made sacrifices of the pure animals after the flood.[179] Why exactly does God only want *tahor* ("pure") animals to be sacrificed? Rabbi Hirsch speculates:

> What does טהור [*tahor*] mean? טהור [*tahor*] is related to צהר [*tzohar*], the transparent, the particles of which are homogenous, and allow rays of light to pass through them. So that טהור [*tahor*] is receptive, that which allows God's rays to pass through, offers no resistance to them … Its opposite is טמא [*tamei*]; closed up, non-receptive to the godly.[180]

Rabbi Hirsch points out that the first dietary commandment of the Torah referring to animal food is in the instructions given to Noah after he stepped off the ark.[181] Among a series of civil injunctions, God states:

> Every moving thing that lives shall be food for you. And as I gave you the green plants, I give you everything. But you shall not eat flesh with its life, that is, its blood. (Genesis 9:3–4)

Man's relationship to the animal kingdom changed drastically after the flood. Not only would the fear and dread of humankind be on all creatures, but man was now permitted to eat of their flesh. No mention is made of distinguishing between pure and impure. He was permitted to eat from "every moving thing."

God gave only one stipulation: man was not to "eat of the flesh with its life, that is, its blood." At face value, this seems to indicate that consuming meat with the blood still in it is forbidden, which is akin to instructions we find in the later books of the Torah.[182] However, the Rabbis who formulated the seven Noachide laws interpreted this differently. They saw it as a prohibition against eating the flesh of a living animal, which is called in Hebrew *ever min ha-chai* (אֵבֶר מִן הַחַי). In other words, the Noachide laws permit a Gentile to eat any flesh except "living flesh or the flesh and blood of a human being."[183] Some authorities hold the opinion that Gentiles must not eat "the flesh of a dead animal unless killed for the specific purpose of eating its flesh."[184] Despite the fact that rabbinic law does not prohibit Gentiles from consuming blood, a few authorities recommend that Gentiles eat only kosher-slaughtered meat in order to be certain that the flesh was not cut from an animal that was still living or twitching.[185]

Dietary restrictions such as the prohibition against eating flesh taken from a live animal can be seen as a method of enhancing oneself spiritually. According to Chaim Clorfene and Yakov Rogalsky, this prohibition "serves as a hint to the potential refinement that man can attain through his eating habits and by practicing kindness to God's creatures."[186] Rabbi Bindman elaborates on this point:

> There is a saying that "What you eat, you are," and the Torah therefore tells the non-Jew also that as long as his food has nothing in it which could go against this one condition, then his eating will enhance and sustain his true personal standing. These requirements for Jews and non-Jews have to do with the spiritual constitution and not with physical health or hygiene or any other scientific fact.[187]

Given this reasoning, we can see that what one chooses to eat has a spiritual effect, no matter if the person is Jewish or Gentile.

## The Stranger and Kosher

So far we have examined dietary laws that are universal in scope and that God gave all mankind to obey. However, the bulk of the dietary laws that we find in Scripture from Mount Sinai onward are specifically given to the Jewish people. At the end of the long list of pure and impure animals in Leviticus 11, God states that these dietary restrictions are to sanctify Israel as a nation: "Consecrate yourselves therefore, and be holy, for I am holy" (Leviticus 11:44). Thus the Mosaic dietary code has an effect similar to the "sign commandments"—that is to say, commandments that are specifically given to Israel as a mark of distinction. Indeed, the kosher diet has helped keep the Jewish people separate and distinct from the nations around them throughout history.

But what kind of relationship might a Gentile have with these laws? We can approach this question by examining the Torah concept of the *ger* (גֵּר).

*Ger* is usually translated as "stranger" or "sojourner" and refers to the non-Israelites who are dwelling among the children of Israel. This ranges from the casual passerby to the Gentile family who makes their permanent home among Israel. They did not necessarily officially become Israelites per se, but rather chose for various reasons to associate closely with them. Non-Jews first appeared among Israel during the Exodus where they voluntarily chose to leave Egypt as companions of the Jewish people.[188] Unlike many other nations of the ancient Near East, "strangers" in Israel enjoyed the Torah's protection, which provided them with economic support, rest on the Sabbath,[189] and freedom from exploitation.[190]

By the time of the late Second Temple period, the term *ger* typically referred to a proselyte—a person who had made a formal conversion to Judaism and was no longer considered a Gentile.[191] These proselytes would then have been under full obligation to keep the Torah in the same manner as the natural-born Jews. This is most likely how the apostles would have interpreted *ger* as well.[192]

However, for the moment, let's examine the dietary obligations of the *ger* as it is understood by most non-rabbinical scholars today, simply as a non-Jewish sojourner.

In some cases it is apparent that the *ger* has the same dietary requirements as the Israelite. For example, Leviticus 17:12 forbids the *ger* from consuming blood. However, in other cases the *ger* has a different standard:

> You shall not eat anything that has died naturally. You may give it to the sojourner [*ger*] who is within your towns, that he may eat it, or you may sell it to a foreigner. For you are a people holy to the LORD your God. You shall not boil a young goat in its mother's milk. (Deuteronomy 14:21)

In this case, a *ger* may eat something that an Israelite is explicitly forbidden to eat.[193] We also find no indication in the texts of Leviticus 11 and Deuteronomy 14 that a *ger* would be required to observe the laws that prohibit eating certain species. Thus, the Torah makes a distinction between the obligations of the foreigner or sojourner and those of the natural born Israelite. A detailed analysis of the concept of the *ger* is beyond the scope of this study. However, even a face-value examination of the *ger* in the Torah shows that the Torah distinguishes between the dietary obligations of Jews and Gentiles.

### Acts 15: The Jerusalem Council

Acts 15 is a pivotal text for Gentile believers in Yeshua and their obligations to *kashrut*. The Jerusalem Council debates whether or not Gentiles who have come to faith in Messiah should be required to become Jews through conversion, which would obligate them to the whole Torah. After a long and heated debate, a verdict is reached. James the Just states:

> Therefore my judgment is that we should not trouble those of the Gentiles who turn to God, but should write to them to abstain from the things polluted by idols, and from sexual immorality, and from what has been strangled, and from blood.[194] For from ancient generations Moses has had in every city those who proclaim him, for he is read every Sabbath in the synagogues. (Acts 15:19–21)

The council decided that they should not be required to convert and thus were not obligated to keep the laws of the Torah in the same way Jews were. Instead, they were given four directives:

1. Abstain from things polluted by idols
2. Abstain from sexual immorality
3. Abstain from what has been strangled
4. Abstain from blood

Some scholars feel that this list represents a sort of proto-Noachide law.[195] During the second Temple period, the rabbis still debated the actual list of universal commandments binding on all humanity, and it seems likely that the apostles interpreted the instructions of Genesis 9:4 as forbidding blood rather than the flesh of a living animal. This also might explain the last line about Moses being preached in the synagogue. In others words, these four things are included in what was already being prescribed in the synagogue for all nations.

Some scholars have speculated that these rulings were not universally binding or that they were only applicable to Gentiles who lived in a Jewish community. Nonetheless, it makes sense to view these instructions as a halachic ruling applying to all Gentile followers of Yeshua. The apostles were given "the keys to kingdom of heaven" and the right to "bind" and "loose," which are terms for making halachic determinations.[196] Richard Baukbaum comments:

> This tradition of direction and communication from the centre is the background to the letter in Acts 15:23–29, which communicates a major halakhic decision of the Jerusalem Christian leadership, assumed to have universal authority on such a matter, to (in this case) Gentile members of churches in the Diaspora.[197]

These rulings are important for our discussion because three of the four prohibitions are dietary in nature.[198]

## Things Contaminated by Idols

Judaism strongly forbids eating food that has been offered to idols. This is explained in detail in the section entitled "Food Offered to Idols." The apostles make it clear that Gentiles are subject to this prohibition as well.

Eating food contaminated by idols is such an important prohibition to the apostolic community that it is brought up again in the book of Revelation.[199] It is also spoken against in early church literature such as the *Didache* and Justin Martyr's *Dialogue with Trypho the Jew* and by no less influential characters in the early church than Clement of Alexandria, Irenaeus, Tertullian, and the fifth-century church father Augustine.[200]

## Things Strangled and Blood

The remaining two dietary prohibitions of the Jerusalem Council both deal with the same issue: the kosher slaughter of meat.

The first is to abstain from "what is strangled." As explained in the section entitled "Abstaining from Blood," the prohibition of "strangled meat" refers to meat that has been improperly slaughtered. This is directly related to the prohibition against "blood":

> The prohibition of "blood" came under the same requirement, referring to the consumption of the blood of animals in any form. These three requirements [abstention from food sacrificed to idols, things strangled, and blood] were thus all ritual, dealing with matters of clean and unclean food.[201]

The fourth prohibition of blood is thus connected to the prohibition of strangulation, since without proper slaughter the blood remains in the meat.

Church history scholar Oskar Skarsaune finds evidence in early church literature that Christians in France still purchased kosher-slaughtered meat even after the church had begun severing its ties from Judaism:

> Under torture, a girl named Biblias in a sudden burst of indignation said, "How can those eat children, who are forbidden to eat the blood even of brute beasts?" This clearly indicates that the community of Lyons [France] still observed the apostolic decree of Acts 15 concerning kosher meat. As Frend aptly remarks, "the question arises, where did the Christians get their meat from? The only possible answer is, from a kosher market established for the Jews, and this in turn indicates fairly close personal relations between the Jews and Christians in the City."[202]

From this we can see that as late as the end of the second century there were still followers of Yeshua who observed the strict prohibition against blood consumption and only ate kosher-slaughtered meat.

Unlike food sacrificed to idols, blood-free meat is a real issue in our modern world. Today most meat found at a grocery store or restaurant is slaughtered without any concern for removing all of the blood. In fact, the two primary methods of killing animals in slaughterhouses, bolt stunning and electrocution, actually cause the retention of some of the animal's blood. Some consider blood left in the meat a delicacy. By purchasing certified kosher meat,

Gentiles are able to observe the prohibition of consuming blood while honoring the Jewish people who preserved this Torah practice for thousands of years. It is also an opportunity for Gentiles to connect and interact with the Jewish community as they find sources of kosher meat.

## Going Further

The only dietary requirements that the ruling in Acts 15 places upon Gentiles are refraining from food sacrificed to idols and eating only kosher-slaughtered meat. Maintaining the distinction between Jews and Gentiles, the apostles did not obligate Gentiles to observe the bulk of the dietary laws given at Mount Sinai. However, there are some compelling reasons why a person who is not Jewish might want to take on more aspects of kosher observance.

To begin with, if we interpret the instructions of the Jerusalem Council as calling for kosher-slaughtered meat, it is hard to believe that the apostles would have imagined setting up *shechitah* for swine and other animals that are not kosher. If a person only eats kosher-slaughtered meat, then they will normally be limited to kosher species of animals. This might suggest that it was already obvious to the apostolic community that Gentiles should only eat kosher species; at the very least, the Council seems to be pushing them in this direction.

It should be pointed out that the apostles set these standards as a minimum threshold of dietary law, not a maximum. They pointed the new Gentile believers in the direction of the Torah's higher standards by encouraging them to remain in the synagogues and learn Torah from the weekly readings:

> For from ancient generations Moses has had in every city those who proclaim him, for he is read every Sabbath in the synagogues. (Acts 15:21)

Thus as the Gentiles were attending synagogue, they would be learning more about the ways of Torah and the kosher diet given to the Jewish people.

The Master and his disciples all ate kosher; many of the new Gentile believers, such as Cornelius, were God-Fearers and would have been keeping a kosher diet on some level as well.[203] When

Gentiles keep kosher they are not only connecting with Yeshua but also with practices of the very earliest non-Jewish believers.

Evidence of this attitude appears in an early Jewish-Christian document called the *Didache*. Written in the late first to early second century, it purports to contain instructions for Gentiles from the twelve apostles. The *Didache* offers some instructions regarding *kashrut*:

> If you can carry the whole yoke of the Lord, you will be perfect; but if you cannot, then do what you can. Concerning food, bear what you can, but carefully keep away from food sacrificed to idols, for it is a worship-service to gods from the realm of the dead. (*Didache* 6:2–3)

"Yoke of the Lord" here refers to the Torah. The *Didache* calls for Gentiles "to do their best to eat food that is kosher—at the very least avoid eating meat that had been offered to idols."[204] Eating kosher was seen as the ideal, but room was made for those who would be unable to bear that yoke.

Although Yeshua himself gives no instructions to Gentiles about keeping kosher, we might draw some conclusions from the story where he casts demons into the herd of pigs.[205] The farmer who raised these pigs must have endured a substantial financial loss as a result of what happened. Since Jews were forbidden to raise swine for any reason, even if they did not consume them,[206] it is likely that the farmer was a Gentile. The story teaches us a lesson about the relationship between impure animals and the spiritual world. The pigs' impurity corresponds to the impurity of the evil spirits.

In the Master's parable of the great catch, he uses "good" (that is, kosher) fish to represent "the righteous" and "bad" (non-kosher) fish to represent "the evil."[207] This correlates to the view that the characteristics of non-kosher animals, which are often scavengers and predators, correlate to evil character traits and behaviors.

The rabbis make similar analogies. For example, they use the swine to illustrate hypocrisy because it has the outward signs of being kosher (split hooves) but not the inward (chewing its cud).

> When [a pig] is lying down, he spreads out his hooves as if to say, "I am pure!" In the same way, this wicked [Roman]

Empire robs and exploits, while trying to appear as if it were executing justice. (*Genesis Rabbah* 65:1)

These spiritual lessons are just as apt for a Gentile as they are for a Jew.

But observing commandments can be more than simply an object lesson. Gentiles can benefit spiritually by voluntarily taking on commandments from the Torah. The Rambam writes that a Gentile who observes additional *mitzvot* beyond what he is obligated to will "receive reward."[208] Surely this principle extends to *kashrut*. The Midrash states:

> Our Rabbis say: In the future, the blessed Holy One will send a herald to announce, "Let anyone who has never eaten the flesh of a pig in his life come and receive his reward. Many people from the nations of the world who have never eaten the flesh of a pig in their lives will come and receive their reward. (*Ecclesiastes Rabbah* 1:28)

Jewish law permits Gentiles to observe additional aspects of *kashrut* as long as one acknowledges that it is voluntary:

> If an individual wishes to accept upon himself a restriction [e.g., eating pork, or shellfish, combinations of milk and meat] in order to gain a practical benefit or to refine his personality, then he is not establishing the restriction as if it were a prohibition for him that is commanded from God, and it is permitted.[209]

As we have already seen, the Torah teaches us that our diets are directly connected to our spiritual lives. As Lauren Winner writes, "a cosmology and an ethics underpin each injunction; to keep kosher is to infuse the simple act of feeding oneself with meaning and consequence."[210]

By keeping kosher, Gentiles in Messianic Jewish communities also help to create a conducive and hospitable environment for Jews who are present. Gentiles who attend Messianic Jewish congregations should adhere to the congregational standards of *kashrut* in the congregation. They should also find ways to accommodate kosher-keeping Jews who visit their homes. In mixed marriages, a

Gentile would do well to keep kosher to the same extent as his or her Jewish spouse.

In summary there are some very compelling reasons for Gentiles to go further in pursuing a kosher diet:

- The apostles' injunctions of Acts 15 point Gentiles in the direction of the Torah's higher standards of *kashrut.*

- The *Didache* encourages Gentiles to embrace as much of a kosher lifestyle as they can.

- It gives non-Jews a sense of solidarity and point of connection with Jewish people.

- It fosters a sense of unity with the Master as well as his earliest Jewish and non-Jewish disciples.

- The actual physical practice of *kashrut* helps instill in the practitioner important spiritual lessons.

- It is a Biblical spiritual discipline that brings blessing and reward.

- A kosher diet can infuse the simple act of eating with godliness.

## Practical Application

The laws of *kashrut* are quite complex and detailed, and they require a substantial commitment. At bare minimum, Gentiles should meet the dietary standard set by Acts 15 and provide their Jewish brothers and sisters with kosher food in their homes. Many Gentile believers who read this may be inspired to go beyond the minimum standard and pursue more elements of a kosher diet. A Gentile who makes this choice should keep in mind a few considerations:

- Do not let other commandments—particularly those that are obligatory—fall by the wayside because of keeping kosher.

- Remember that *kashrut* serves to bring distinction and identity to the Jewish people. Since keeping kosher is so closely linked with Jewish identity, a

Gentile should be careful to avoid giving others the impression by his observance that he is Jewish.

- Do not criticize or judge another person for keeping a lesser kosher standard. This is especially the case if the other person is a Gentile who has no legal dietary obligation beyond Acts 15.

- As best as possible, keep in step with other members of your community and be an encouragement to others.

- With each decision you make regarding *kashrut*, prayerfully seek God's leading.

## Conclusion

Keeping kosher can be of benefit for both Jews and Gentiles. The concept of being careful about what we eat is universal and time-less. Gentiles may find that a simplified, balanced approach will enable them to enjoy some of the spiritual benefits of keeping kosher, accommodate Jewish guests, and interact with the Jewish community while creating the fewest obstacles possible for family and friends who are not Jewish and upholding the uniqueness of the Jewish people.

May you be blessed in your journey of spiritual eating!

# REFERENCE
# MATERIAL

# BIBLIOGRAPHY

Bauckham, Richard, ed. *The Book of Acts in its First Century Setting, Volume 4: Palestinian Setting.* Grand Rapids, MI: Eerdmans, 1995.

Bindman, Yirmeyahu. *The Seven Colors of the Rainbow: Torah Ethics for Non-Jews.* Colorado Springs, CO: Schueller House, 1995.

Burdock, George A. *Encyclopedia of Food and Color Additives.* 3 volumes. Boca Raton, FL: CRC Press, 1997.

Campo, Juan E. "Dietary Laws," *Encyclopedia of Islam.* New York: Facts On File, 2009.

Clorfene, Chaim, and Yakov Rogalsky. T*he Path of the Righteous Gentile.* Southfield, MI: Targum Press, 1987.

Cohen, Abraham. *Everyman's Talmud: The Major Teachings of the Rabbinic Sages.* New York: Schocken, 1995.

Crown, Alan David, Reinhard Pummer, and Abraham Tal. *A Companion to Samaritan Studies.* Tübingen, Germany: Mohr-Siebeck, 1993.

Davies, William David, Louis Finkelstein, and Steven T. Katz. *The Cambridge History of Judaism: The Late Roman-Rabbinic Period.* New York: Cambridge University Press, 2006.

Eby, Aaron. "Rashbatz and the New Testament." *Messiah Journal* 103 (Spring 2010/5770): 58–62.

Eisenberg, Ronald L. *The JPS Guide to Jewish Traditions.* Philadelphia: Jewish Publication Society, 2004.

Etheridge, J. W. *The Targums of Onkelos and Jonathan ben Uzziel on the Pentateuch, with the Fragments of the Jerusalem Targum.* London: Longman, Green, Longman, and Roberts, 1862-1865.

Felix, Yehudah. *Kil'ei Zera'im Veharkavah.* Tel Aviv: Devir, 1967.

Fishkoff, Sue. *Kosher Nation.* New York: Schocken, 2010.

Fitzmyer, Joseph A. *The Acts of the Apostles: A New Translation with Introduction and Commentary.* New York: Yale University Press, 1998.

Flusser, David. *Judaism and the Origins of Christianity.* Jerusalem: The Magnes Press, 1988.

Forst, Binyomin. *The Laws of Kashrus.* Brooklyn, NY: Mesorah Publications, 2004.

Fox, Patrick F., Timothy P. Guinee, Timothy M. Cogan, and Paul L. H. McSweeney. *Fundamentals of Cheese Science.* Gaithersburg, MD: Aspen Publishers, 2000.

Gillespie, James R., and Frank B. Flanders. *Modern Livestock and Poultry Production.* Clifton Park, NY: Cengage Learning, 2009.

Greene, Velvl. "Spiritual Molecules." *B'Or HaTorah* VI (1987):159–164.

Harris, R. Laird, Gleason L. Archer, Jr., and Bruce K. Waltke, editors. *Theological Wordbook of the Old Testament.* 2 volumes. Chocago: Moody Press, 1980.

Herczeg, Yisrael Isser Zvi. *The Torah: With Rashi's Commentary Translated, Annotated, and Elucidated .* Brooklyn, NY: Mesorah Publications, 1999.

Hirsch, Samson Raphael. *The Pentateuch.* 6 volumes. Gateshead, Scotland: Judaica Press, 1999.

Johnson, H. H. "The Acts, XV. 29." *The Classical Review* 33:5/6 (August/September 1919): 100–101.

Kinzer, Mark. *Post-Missionary Messianic Judaism.* Grand Rapids: Brazos Press, 2005.

Kitov, Eliyahu. *The Book of Our Heritage: Adar–Nisan.* Translated by Nachman Bulman. Jerusalem: Feldheim, 1997.

Knobel, Peter. "What I Eat Is Who I Am: Kashrut and Identity" in *The Sacred Table: Creating a Jewish Food Ethic.* Edited by Mary L. Lamore. New York: CCAR Press, 2011.

Lancaster, D. Thomas. *The Holy Epistle to the Galatians: Sermons on a Messianic Jewish Approach.* Marshfield,MO: First Fruits of Zion, 2011.

Leibowitz, Nehama. *New Studies in Bereshit (Genesis).* Jerusalem: Hemed Press, 2000.

Levinson, Yaakov. *The Jewish Guide to Natural Nutrition.* Jerusalem, New York: Feldheim, 1995.

Lichtenstein, Aaron. *The Seven Laws of Noah.* New York: Z. Berman Books, 1995.

Lipschutz, Yacov. *Kashruth*. Brooklyn, NY: Mesorah Publications, 1999.

MacDonald, Nathan. *What Did the Ancient Israelites Eat: Diet in Biblical Times*. Grand Rapids, MI: Eerdmans, 2008.

Maloney, Elliot C. *Semitic Interference in Marcan Syntax*. Chico, CA: Scholar's Press, 1981.

Marks, Gil. *Encyclopedia of Jewish Food*. Hoboken, NJ: John Wiley & Sons, 2010.

Milgrom, Jacob. "'You Shall Not Boil a Kid in Its Mother's Milk': An Archaeological Myth Destroyed." *Bible Review* 1:03 (Fall 1985): 48–55.

Milgrom, Jacob. *Leviticus 1–16*. New York: Doubleday, 1991.

Miller, Chaim. *The Gutnick Edition Chumash: The Book of Genesis*. Brooklyn, NY; Kol Menachem, 2003.

Miller, Chris A. "Did Peter's Vision in Acts 10 Pertain to Men or the Menu?" *Bibliotheca Sacra* 159:635 (2002): 302–317.

Murray, Michelle. *Playing a Jewish Game: Gentile Christian Judaizing in the First and Second Centuries CE*. Ontario, Canada: Wilfrid Laurier University Press, 2004.

Nanos, Mark D. *The Mystery of Romans: The Jewish Context of Paul's Letter*. Minneapolis: Fortress Press, 1996.

Painter, John. *Mark's Gospel*. London: Routledge, 1997.

Polhill, John B. "The Acts of the Apostles" in *ESV Study Bible*. Edited by Lane T. Dennis et al. Wheaton, IL: Crossway Bibles, 2008.

Polhill, John B. *The New American Commentary: Acts*. Nashville, TN: Broadman Press 1992.

Reichenberg, Shaul. *The Procedure for Setting Aside T'rumot and Ma'asrot*. Jerusalem: Feldheim, 1997.

Sarna, Nahum. *The JPS Torah Commentary: Genesis*. New York: Jewish Publication Society, 1989.

Sasson, Jack M. "Should Cheeseburgers Be Kosher?" *Bible Review*, December 2003. Cited 13 July 2011. Online: http://www.basarchive.org/sample/bswbBrowse.asp?PubID=BSBR&Volume=19&Issue=6&ArticleID=5.

Scherman, Nosson, and Meir Zlotowitz. *The Stone Edition Tanach*. Brooklyn, NY: Mesorah, 1998.

Scherman, Nosson. *Zemiros and Bircas Hamazon*. Brooklyn, NY: Mesorah, 1998.

Schwartz, Yoel. "Noahide Commandments," in *Service from the Heart*. Edited by Rabbi Michael Katz et al. Rose, OK: Oklahoma B'nai Noah Society, 2007.

Skarsaune, Oskar. *In the Shadow of the Temple.* Downers Grove, IL: InterVarsity Press, 2002.

Smith, Mark S. *The Rituals and Myths of the Feast of the Goodly Gods of KTU/CAT 1.23.* Atlanta: Society of Biblical Literature, 2006.

Steinsaltz, Adin. *The Essential Talmud.* Translated by Chaya Galai. London: Weidenfeld and Nicolson, 1976.

Steinsaltz, Adin. *The Talmud: A Reference Guide.* New York: Random House, 1989.

Tigay, Jeffery. *JPS Torah Commentary: Deuteronomy.* Philadelphia: Jewish Publication Society, 1996.

Tomson, Peter J. *Paul and the Jewish Law: Halakha in the Letters of the Apostle to the Gentiles.* Minneapolis: Fortress Press, 1990.

Vamosh, Miriam Feinberg. *Food at the Time of the Bible.* Herzlia, Israel: Palphot, 2006.

Weiner, Moshe. *The Divine Code.* Jerusalem: Ask Noah International, 2011.

Winner, Lauren F. *Mudhouse Sabbath: An Invitation to Spiritual Discipline.* Brewster, MA: Paraclete Press, 2010.

Witherington, Ben, III. *The Gospel of Mark: a Socio-Rhetorical Commentary.* Grand Rapids: Eerdmans, 2001.

# GLOSSARY

Here are some terms used in this book along with others that you might run into when studying about *kashrut*. Since these terms are from other languages, they can be spelled a number of ways.

| | | |
|---|---|---|
| *akathartos* | (Greek) | impure; Greek equivalent of tamei |
| *Ashkenazi* | | Relating to eastern European Jewish communities and culture. |
| *basar* | (Hebrew) | Meat, containing meat products. Hebrew equivalent of *fleishig*. |
| *basmala* | (Arabic) | An invocation of the name of God performed during certain Islamic rituals. |
| *behemah* | (Hebrew) | animals; depending on the context, either large land animals in general or domesticated animals. |
| *bishul akum* | (Hebrew) | certain foods that are not considered kosher simply because they are cooked by Gentiles |
| *chalav* | (Hebrew) | Milk; dairy; containing dairy products. Hebrew equivalent of *milchig* |
| *chalav stam* | (Hebrew) | Milk that is kosher but does not meet the strict requirements of *chalav yisra'el*. |

| | | |
|---|---|---|
| *chalav yisrael* or *cholov yisroel* | (Hebrew) | Dairy products that are produced completely under the supervision of observant Jews. |
| *chametz* | (Hebrew) | Food that is prohibited on Passover. |
| *chelev* | (Hebrew) | fat portions, which may not be eaten from cows, sheep, or goats |
| *chullin* | (Hebrew) | non-consecrated, normal foods |
| *de'oraita* | (Aramaic) | of biblical origin or authority |
| *derabbanan* | (Aramaic) | of rabbinic origin or authority |
| *fleishig* or *fleishedik* | (Yiddish) | Containing meat products, which means that it cannot be combined with dairy. |
| *gid hanasheh* | (Hebrew) | the sciatic nerve, which may not be eaten |
| *glatt* | (Yiddish) | literally, "smooth;" meat from animals that are free from certain internal defects; colloquially (and incorrectly), strictly kosher |
| *halachah* | (Hebrew) | Jewish law. |
| *halal* | (Arabic) | literally, "legally permitted." Food that is permitted according to Islamic law. |
| *hechsher* | (Hebrew) | a symbol from a supervising agency assuring consumers that a product is kosher |
| *kashering* | | making something kosher, such as dishes that may have been contaminated by non-kosher food |
| *kashrut* or *kashrus* | (Hebrew) | the concept or application of dietary law in Judaism. |
| *katharizo* | (Greek) | to purify. |

| | | |
|---|---|---|
| *kil'ayim* | (Hebrew) | a forbidden mixture, such as two crops in the same field |
| *kitniyot or kitniyos* | (Hebrew) | literally, "small things"; additional items that some authorities forbid on Passover |
| *kodesh* | (Hebrew) | a consecrated item such as a sacrifice |
| *koinos* | (Greek) | common, non-holy; Greek equivalent of *chullin.* |
| *kosher or kasher* | (Hebrew) | literally, "fitting, acceptable, appropriate"; usually used to describe food that may be eaten according to Jewish law |
| *ma'aser* | (Hebrew) | tithe |
| *mashgiach* | (Hebrew) | an expert in kashrut who oversees and approves food production such as in a factory or restaurant |
| *matzah* | (Hebrew) | flat, typically cracker-like bread that is made without leaven or fermentation |
| *mehadrin* | (Hebrew) | literally, "beautified"; acceptable according to meticulous standards in regard to Jewish law |
| *metzora* | (Hebrew) | a person afflicted with *tzara'at.* |
| *milchig or milchedik* | (Yiddish) | containing dairy products, which means that it cannot be combined with meat |
| *mitzvah/mitzvot (mitzvos)* | (Hebrew) | commandment/s |
| *neta reva'i* | (Hebrew) | literally, "fourth year planting"; fruit from a tree in its fourth year, which has a special holy status |

| | | |
|---|---|---|
| *nevelah* | (Hebrew) | literally, "spoiled"; the carcass of an animal that died from something other than kosher slaughter |
| *orlah* | (Hebrew) | fruit from a tree during its first three years, which may not be eaten; in other contexts, foreskin |
| *pareve or parve* | (Hebrew/Yiddish) | containing neither meat nor dairy products |
| *reva'i* | (Hebrew) | an abbreviated term for *neta reva'i* |
| *se'or* | (Hebrew) | an inedible lump of dough with a high yeast content that is used to leaven other dough |
| *Sephardi* | | relating to Mediterranean Jewish communities and culture |
| *shechitah* | (Hebrew) | slaughter of animals in accordance with Jewish law |
| *sheretz* | (Hebrew) | vermin; a category of animals whose carcasses transmit ritual impurity, such as rodents or reptiles |
| *shmittah* | (Hebrew) | the seventh "sabbatical" year, in which food in Israel must not be planted nor harvested |
| *shochet* | (Hebrew) | an expert trained in the proper method of slaughter according to Jewish law |
| *tahor* | (Hebrew) | ritually pure |
| *tamei* | (Hebrew) | ritually impure |
| *tehorah* | (Hebrew) | ritual purity |
| *treif* | (Yiddish) | Literally, "torn"; anything that is not kosher; from the Hebrew word *treifah* |

| | | |
|---|---|---|
| *treifah* | (Hebrew) | literally, "torn"; an animal with a life-threatening injury or defect |
| *tum'ah* | (Hebrew) | ritual impurity or contamination |
| *tzara'at* | (Hebrew) | a biblical skin disease often translated as "leprosy" which causes ritual impurity |
| *vaad* | (Hebrew) | "committee," often a board of kosher overseers |

# SCRIPTURE REFERENCE INDEX

# SUBJECT INDEX

# U

# V

# ENDNOTES

1   Binyomin Forst, *The Laws of Kashrus* (Brooklyn: Mesorah Publications, 2004), 24.

2   Nathan MacDonald, *What Did the Ancient Israelites Eat: Diet in Biblical Times* (Grand Rapids: Eerdmans, 2008), 87, 101.

3   Mark Kinzer, *Post Missionary Messianic Judaism* (Grand Rapids: Brazos Press, 2005), 151.

4   D. Thomas Lancaster, *The Holy Epistle to the Galatians: Sermons on a Messianic Jewish Approach* (Marshfield, Missouri: First Fruits of Zion, 2011), 189–190.

5   Peter Knobel, "What I Eat Is Who I Am: Kashrut and Identity" in *The Sacred Table: Creating a Jewish Food Ethic* (ed. Mary L. Lamore; New York: CCAR Press, 2011), 442–443.

6   Kinzer, *Post Missionary Messianic Judaism*, 58. (Emphasis from the original author.)

7   For example, see m.*Shevu'ot* 3:6; m.*Avot* 4:9.

8   Compare 1 John 3:4.

9   See Isaiah 65:4; 66:17.

10  See Numbers 19:11–22.

11  See Leviticus 7:20–21.

12  See Leviticus 11:39, 17:15; Deuteronomy 14:21.

13  See, for example, 1 Maccabees 1:47, 62.

14  *Legei* is present tense, "He says," but in narrative is often translated as past tense.

15  John Painter, *Mark's Gospel* (London: Routledge, 1997), 8.

16  Ben Witherington III, *The Gospel of Mark: A Socio-Rhetorical Commentary* (Grand Rapids: Eerdmans, 2001), 19.

17  See Elliot C. Maloney, *Semitic Interference in Marcan Syntax* (Chico, California: Scholar's Press, 1981).

18    See *Mishneh Torah, Sefer Taharah, Hilchot Tum'at Ochalin* 16:8: "Everything that is written in Torah and tradition about the laws of ritual purity and impurity refer only to the sanctuary and its sacrifices (*kodesh*), contributions to the priesthood (*trumah*), and second tithe (*ma'aser sheni*). It prohibits those who are *tamei* from entering the sanctuary or eating *kodesh* or *trumah* or *ma'aser* in a state of impurity. But as for *chullin*, there is no such prohibition. Rather, it is permitted to eat *chullin* that is *tamei* and to drink beverages that are *tamei*."

19    If so, what do we make of Ezekiel 4:12–15? Commentators explain this as a prophetic parable. Neither human dung nor cow dung would make his food *tamei*, but the repulsiveness of dung *symbolizes* the impurity of Israel in exile. As a priest, it would be problematic for Ezekiel actually to contaminate himself.

20    The leaders at the time decreed a fast in response to the tragedy (m. *Ta'anit* 3:6).

21    See Numbers 19:21.

22    NIV Study Bible, p. 1667 (Acts 10:15).

23    John B. Polhill, "The Acts of the Apostles" in *ESV Study Bible* (eds. Lane T. Dennis et al.; Wheaton, Ill.: Crossway Bibles, 2008), 2103.

24    The term often translated "circumcision party" literally means "those of the circumcision." This is simply a term for "Jews" and does not necessarily mean that they were an organized faction.

25    Leviticus Rabbah 13:5.

26    There are a few other related concepts in Jewish law, such as *gevinat akum* ("cheese of idolaters"), and *yein nesech* ("libation wine"). It is likely that many of these prohibitions were formalized after the destruction of the Temple in 70 CE and would not even apply in Peter's time. But if they did, they would still only prove a minor inconvenience and would not prevent a conscientious and hospitable Gentile from being able to provide kosher meals.

27    Lichtenstein, commentary on Acts 10:15, footnote.

28    Malbim, commentary on Ezekiel 4:14.

29    Ibid.

30    Some translations render the verse, "… and I will not come into the city."

31    Rashi, commentary on b. *Ta'anit* 11b.

32    I.e., it bears a slight resemblance. One-sixtieth has significance in Jewish law in that it is considered barely beyond the threshold of perception. For example, food that accidentally becomes contaminated by a non-kosher ingredient is still considered kosher if the proportion is less than one-sixtieth, because the taste is nullified

by the majority. By calling the Sabbath "one-sixtieth part of the age to come," it expresses that it represents a barely discernable hint of what the future world is like.

33 b.*Brachot* 57b.

34 Nosson Scherman, *Zemiros and Bircas Hamazon* (Brooklyn: Mesorah, 1998), 73. Scherman writes that *Mah Yedidus* was written by an unknown author named Menachem, and it was first printed in 5305 AM (1544–1545 CE).

35 This passage of the Talmud continues by comparing a wife to the Torah, to a protective city wall, and peace.

36 m.*Yevamot* 7:6.

37 In the humorous song "The Reluctant Cannibal" on the album *At the Drop of a Hat* by Flanders and Swann (c. 1956), a savage tribesman uses a comparable argument to refute his son who refuses to engage in cannibalism: "But people have always eaten people, what else is there to eat? If the Juju had meant us not to eat people, he wouldn't have made us of meat!"

38 Abraham Cohen, *Everyman's Talmud: The Major Teachings of the Rabbinic Sages* (New York: Schocken, 1995), 230.

39 The "sin of desecration" (Hebrew: *me'ilah*, מְעִילָה) normally refers to unlawful use of consecrated property, such as items belonging to the Temple or priesthood.

40 Peter J. Tomson, *Paul and the Jewish Law: Halakha in the Letters of the Apostle to the Gentiles* (Minneapolis: Fortress Press, 1990), 242.

41 Mark D. Nanos, *The Mystery of Romans: The Jewish Context of Paul's Letter* (Minneapolis: Fortress Press, 1996) 92.

42 The ESV incorrectly translates *asthenemata* (ἀσθενήματα) as "failings," which could imply culpability on their part. However, the term actually means "weaknesses" or "infirmities," and it does not imply that the "weak" are at fault. If Paul had actually called them "failings," he would ironically be guilty of casting judgment on the weaker brother.

43 One who has taken a vow which entails abstaining from any wine.

44 A Gentile who has accepted the laws that are considered to apply to all humanity, including the prohibition of eating meat from a live animal.

45 Tomson, *Paul and the Jewish Law*, 244.

46 Tomson, *Paul and the Jewish Law*, 244.

47 The rulings in this *mishnah* are not considered to apply in Orthodox Judaism today.

48 *Pesikta DeRav Kahana* 4 (*Parashat Parah*).

49 Ibid.

50    "Kosher" is the Ashkenazi (Eastern European) pronunciation, which is popular in the United States. With a Sephardic accent, the word is pronounced "kasher." This Hebrew word (כָּשֵׁר) appears once in the Bible (Esther 8:5). The study and practice of kosher law is called in Hebrew kashrus (Ashkenazi) or kashrut (Sephardic).

51    Kummer, Corby "High on the Hog," *The New York Times* (August 12, 2005).

52    George A. Burdock, *Encyclopedia of Food and Color Additives* (3 vols.; Boca Raton: CRC Press, 1997), 1:1165.

53    "Vienna® Beef Franks and Sausages," n.p. [cited 13 July 2011]. Online: http://www.viennabeef.com/products/category.asp?CATEGORY_ID=2.

54    Herrman, Matt. "Do You Know What's on Your Plate?" *The Michigan Daily* (September 26, 2001).

55    Scales on sharks and rays and similar animals are in a category termed "placoid scales."

56    For example, the etymological root of the English word "seminary" comes from the Latin words for ""seed" and "room."

57    For example, although the French word *demande* is related to the English word "demand," it means "request, propose" without any urgent or forceful implication.

58    Ramban, commentary on Leviticus 11:9.

59    "Filet-O-Fish," n.p. [cited 13 July 2011]. Online: http://nutrition.mcdonalds.com/nutritionexchange/itemDetailInfo.do?itemID=5926.

60    "Mystery Fish," *Consumer Reports*, December 2011: 18–22.

61    Jenn Abelson and Beth Daley, "From Sea to Sushi Bar, a System Open to Abuse," *Boston Globe,* October 24, 2011. Cited 31 October 2011. Online: http://articles.boston.com/2011-10-24/business/30317057_1_white-tuna-true-world-foods-escolar.

62    Jenn Abelson and Beth Daley, "'Key West Grouper' in Name Only," *Boston Globe,* October 24, 2011. Cited 31 October 2011. Online: http://www.bostonglobe.com/business/2011/10/23/dish-was-key-west-grouper-name-only/QaPKsqpXokpB6t8zZmy1kJ/story.html

63    Maurice Burton and Robert Burton, "Dogfish," *The International Wildlife Encyclopedia* 10:686–688. [Additional info for bibliography: (Tarrytown, New York: Marshall Cavendish, 2002)]

64    ArtScroll cites R' Saadia and Chizkuni in identifying the *bat haya'anah* (בַּת הַיַּעֲנָה) as the ostrich. Nosson Scherman and Meir Zlotowitz, *The Stone Edition Tanach* (Brooklyn: Mesorah, 1998), 268.

65    "Among the fowls – The true signification of the following Hebrew words is now lost, as the Jews at this day confess; which not falling

out without God's singular providence may intimate the cessation of this law, the exact observation whereof since Christ came is become impossible." Matthew Poole, *Annotations upon the Holy Bible* (London: 1700), cxxvi.

"From our imperfect knowledge of the natural history of Palestine, Arabia, and the contiguous countries at that time, it is not easy to determine exactly what some of the prohibited birds were; although they must have been all well known among the people to whom these laws were given" (Robert Jamieson, Adrew Robert Fausset, David Brown, *A Commentary, Critical and Explanatory, on the Old and New Testaments* (2 vols.; Hartford, CT: S. S. Scranton & Company, 1871), 1:80.

66  There is some dispute about the turkey, but there is a general consensus that it is safe.

67  James R. Gillespie, Frank B. Flanders, *Modern Livestock and Poultry Production* (Clifton Park, New York: Cengage Learning, 2009), 908.

68  Genesis 1:21–22, for example.

69  Ronald L. Eisenberg, *The JPS Guide to Jewish Traditions* (Philadelphia: Jewish Publication Society, 2004), 722.

70  Rambam, *Sefer HaMitzvot*, negative commandment 183.

71  Adin Steinsaltz, *The Talmud: A Reference Guide* (New York: Random House, 1989), 191.

72  Yacov Lipschutz, *Kashruth* (Brooklyn: Mesorah Publications, 1999), 26–27.

73  Jeffery Tigay, *JPS Torah Commentary: Deuteronomy* (Philadelphia: Jewish Publication Society, 1996), 125.

74  b.*Yoma* 75b.

75  Philo, *De specialibus legibus* 4:122. Also compare Joseph and Aseneth 8:5, which uses the term "bread of hanging/strangling" (ἄρτον ἀγχόνης) in reference to idolatrous food.

76  John B. Polhill, *The New American Commentary: Acts* (Nashville, TN: Broadman Press 1992), 330.

77  Joseph A. Fitzmyer, *The Acts of the Apostles: A New Translation with Introduction and Commentary* (New York, NY: Yale University Press, 1998), 557.

78  Tomson, *Paul and the Jewish Law*, 178–179.

79  Bauckham, *The Book of Acts in its First Century Setting, Volume 4: Palestinian Setting*, 459.

80  Code of Federal Regulations, Title 9, Part 313.

81  World Organisation for Animal Health, "Slaughter of Animals" in *Terrestrial Animal Health Code* 7.5.1 [cited 13 July 2011]. Online:

http://www.oie.int/index.php?id=169&L=0&htmfile=chapitre_1.7.5. htm.

82 Trapping could possibly allow a person to kill a wild animal in a permitted manner. Animals might also be hunted for other resources such as hides. But while hunting and trapping are not explicitly forbidden in Judaism, rabbinic literature generally views them negatively, associating them with wicked personalities such as Nimrod and Esau. Hunting for sport is considered inhumane and forbidden.

83 See Genesis 1:30, 2:7, 6:17, 7:15, 7:22, 25:8, 25:17, 35:29, 49:33; Job 12:10, 14:10; Mark 15:37, 15:39; Luke 23:46; Acts 5:5, 5:10, 12:23.

84 Leviticus 11:33, for example.

85 Rashi, commentary on Numbers 31:23.

86 Ramban, commentary on Numbers 31:23.

87 See Numbers 1:20–54.

88 b.*Avodah Zarah* 75b.

89 Joe Brown, "Why New York City's Iconic Pizza Is So Tough to Replicate," *Wired Magazine* 16.05 (April 2008). Cited 13 July 2011. Online: http://www.wired.com/culture/lifestyle/magazine/16-05/ ps_pizzasci.

90 b.*Pesachim* 30b.

91 Yosef Karo, *Shulchan Aruch, Yoreh De'ah* 87:1.

92 Such as *behemah* (a large land animal such as a cow) being translated as "animal."

93 Such as *sheretz* (teeming creatures) being translated as "insects."

94 Such as *ohf* (birds), which includes the bat.

95 Such as "naturally" in Deuteronomy 14:21.

96 Such as "everything that can stand the fire" in Numbers 31:22.

97 Such as "You shall eat no fat" in Leviticus 7:23.

98 Since milk contains a large percentage of water, the boiling point is nearly the same, although the precise temperature would depend on atmospheric pressure.

99 This is the root form. In context of the verse ("You shall not boil") it is written *lo tevashel* (לֹא תְבַשֵּׁל). In each verse, the exact permutation might vary, although the verb itself and its basic meaning is the same. In each verse, notice the root letters (ב-שׁ-ל).

100 In different permutations, only because of their relative positions in the sentence. Nonetheless, the same verb is used in both.

101 Earl S. Kalland, "בָּשַׁל," *TWOT* 1:136–137.

102 Here is another example of a verb with both a general and a specific meaning. Suppose you heard that your favorite author "wrote" a new novel. According to the Merriam-Webster dictionary, the word originates from "Middle English, from Old English *writan* to scratch, draw, inscribe." The first definition of the word is "to form (as characters or symbols) on a surface with an instrument (as a pen)." Does this mean that the author scrawled it with a pen or pencil, rather than typing it on a computer or even dictating it? Again, the point of the statement is not the method of transcription, but that the person authored the book, one of the broader definitions of the term.

103 Judges 14:6; 1 Samuel 10:3; Isaiah 11:6.

104 Yosef Karo, *Shulchan Aruch, Yoreh De'ah* 87:1 (author's translation).

105 In most other places the *LXX* uses the word *erifos*, which does mean "kid."

106 Philo, *De virtutibus* 144.

107 Jacob Milgrom, *Leviticus 1–16* (New York: Doubleday, 1991), 741–742.

108 Miriam Feinberg Vamosh, *Food at the Time of the Bible* (Herzlia, Israel: Palphot, 2006), 67.

109 MacDonald, *What Did the Ancient Israelites Eat*, 35.

110 Here is another example of a specific noun standing in for its general category. Suppose a sign posted in a store reads, "No shirt, no shoes, no service." If a man walks in wearing boots rather than shoes, he will not be asked to leave. Even though boots are not technically shoes, the point of the policy does not have anything to do with the specific type of footwear. (Archaeologists thousands of years in the future that uncover this sign may have a hard time decoding its terse language.)

111 Rashi, commentary on Exodus 21:28.

112 Vamosh, *Food at the Time of the Bible*, 69.

113 MacDonald, *What Did the Ancient Israelites Eat*, 35.

114 Edwin Yamauchi, "חָלָב," *TWOT* 1:285.

115 m.*Chullin* 8:4.

116 m.*Chullin* 8:4.

117 b.*Shabbat* 130a.

118 m.*Chullin* 8:1.

119 Adin Steinsaltz, *The Essential Talmud* (trans. Chaya Galai; London: Weidenfeld and Nicolson, 1976), 189.

120 Another important targum is commonly called *Targum Pseudo-Jonathan*, although its date of origin is probably much later, so I have not included it as an example here. Nonetheless *Targum Pseudo-*

*Jonathan* is even more emphatic about the separation of meat and dairy.

121 While earlier scholars tended to date Targum Onkelos to a later period, modern scholars place it in the Tannaitic period (first and second centuries CE) based on linguistic analysis. See William David Davies, Louis Finkelstein, Steven T. Katz, *The Cambridge History of Judaism: The Late Roman-Rabbinic Period* (New York: Cambridge University Press, 2006), 473.

122 J. W. Etheridge, *The Targums of Onkelos and Jonathan ben Uzziel on the Pentateuch: with the Fragments of the Jerusalem Targum* (London: Longman, Green, Longman, and Roberts, 1862–1865).

123 The Samaritans do not even accept the books of the Prophets and Writings, let alone Oral Law.

124 Alan David Crown, Reinhard Pummer, Abraham Tal, *A Companion to Samaritan Studies* (Tübingen, Germany: Mohr-Siebeck, 1993), 75–76.

125 Deuteronomy 26:9.

126 b.*Shabbat* 130a.

127 Luke 7:36, 11:37, 14:1.

128 b.*Bava Metzia* 86b.

129 Genesis 29:21–28.

130 Leviticus 18:18.

131 Moses Maimonides, *Guide to the Perplexed* 3:48 (Author's translation).

132 Ugarit is the site of an ancient city-state located on the Mediterranean coast.

133 Yamauchi, *TWOT* 1:285.

134 Jack M. Sasson, "Should Cheeseburgers Be Kosher?" *Bible Review,* December 2003. Cited 13 July 2011. Online: http://www.basarchive. org/sample/bswbBrowse.asp?PubID=BSBR&Volume=19&Issue=6&Art icleID=5.

135 Mark S. Smith, *The Rituals and Myths of the Feast of the Goodly Gods of KTU/CAT 1.23* (Atlanta: Society of Biblical Literature, 2006), 52–53.

136 This dish is sometimes transliterated as *leben immo* or other similar combinations.

137 See Jacob Milgrom, "'You Shall Not Boil a Kid in Its Mother's Milk': An Archaeological Myth Destroyed," *Bible Review* 1:3 (Fall 1985): 48–55.

138 Sue Fishkoff, *Kosher Nation* (New York: Schocken, 2010), 168.

139 Fishkoff, *Kosher Nation*, 160.

140 *Sefer HaChinnuch, Mishpatim* 91.

141 Shaul Reichenberg, *The Procedure for Setting Aside T'rumot and Ma'asrot* (Jerusalem: Feldheim 1997), 9.

142  m.*Terumah* 4:3.

143  *Mishnah Berurah* 241:4.

144  This practice has its parallel in Judaism. Today, it is common to set aside a portion of one's income for the poor and needy. This is termed *ma'aser kesafim*, "monetary tithe."

145  Reichenberg, *T'rumot and Ma'asrot*, 26.

146  m.*Kiddushin* 1:9.

147  b.*Kiddushin* 38b.

148  m.*Orlah* 3:9.

148  b.*Kiddushin* 54b.

150  b.*Brachot* 35a. This is based on the use of the term "yield" (*tevu'ah*, תְּבוּאָה) which is associated elsewhere with grapevines.

151  Akiva Wolff, "Jewish Perspectives on Genetic Engineering." *Jewish Environmental Perspectives* 2 (October 2001). Cited 23 September 2011. Online: http://www.jcpa.org/art/jep2.htm.

152  Sometimes people interpret the prohibition of *kil'ayim* as a ban on manipulating creation. However, this does not follow logically, since planting two crops in the same field does not change the actual species at all. A natural, unfarmed meadow is likely to contain a mixture of plant species. It is only in a man-made, cultivated field in which species are neatly separated into quadrants and rows. And yet it is this unnatural, manipulated state that God instructs us to create.

Man was placed in the Garden of Eden to tend it. He was purposely invested with creative powers and enjoined to cooperate with God in the creative process. The most highly processed foods of the ancient world were wine and bread. These were considered special because they represent the cooperation between God and man. While man must use his creative abilities wisely and carefully, it is not appropriate to add to the commandments by interpreting the prohibition of *kil'ayim* as a ban on anything artificial.

153  Rambam, *Mishneh Torah, Hilchot Kil'ayim* 5:3.

154  Juan E. Campo, "Dietary Laws," *Encyclopedia of Islam* (New York: Facts On File, 2009), 198.

155  Some assert that the Allah of Islam was originally the moon god named Sin of pre-Islamic Arabian peoples. While many groups in the Ancient Near East worshiped the moon, this is not really relevant. Islamic teaching is clear that Allah created all things and is not a moon god. Even if pagans called a moon god Allah (or a variation thereof), that should not be surprising, since Allah just means "god." In the same way, Canaanites worshiped a god they called El, which is also a word for the God of Israel in the Bible.

156 Quran 5:5.

157 *Code of Federal Regulations*, Title 21, Volume 3, Part 173.275.

158 Patrick F. Fox, Timothy P. Guinee, Timothy M. Cogan, and Paul L. H. McSweeney, *Fundamentals of Cheese Science* (Gaithersburg, Maryland: Aspen Publishers, 2000), 130–131.

159 m.*Avodah Zarah* 2:5.

160 b.*Avodah Zarah* 29b, 35a–b.

161 Gil Marks, "Chametz," *Encyclopedia of Jewish Food* (Hoboken: John Wiley & Sons, 2010), 101–102.

162 Found in m.*Challah* 1:1.

163 Gil Marks, "Chametz," 101–102.

164 Yehudah Felix, *Kil'ei Zera'im Veharkavah* (Tel Aviv: Devir, 1967), 22–33.

165 m.*Kilayim* 1:1.

166 b.*Pesachim* 46a.

167 Eliyahu Kitov, *The Book of Our Heritage: Adar–Nisan* (trans. Nachman Bulman; Jerusalem: Feldheim, 1997), 490–491.

168 The sages debated over whether or not Adam was permitted to eat the meat from animals that died by themselves (b.*Sanhedrin* 59b). See Aaron Lichtenstein, *The Seven Laws of Noah* (New York, NY: Z. Berman Books, 1995), 54-55.

169 Rabbi Chaim Miller, *The Gutnick Edition Chumash: The Book of Genesis* (Brooklyn, NY; Kol Menachem, 2003), 13.

170 *Kovetz Tzimchonut V'HaShalom* 31.

171 For example James the Just (Hegesippus in Eusebius' *History of the Church* 2:23), Matthew (Clement of Alexandria, *The Instructor* 2:1), and Peter (*Clementine Homilies* 12:6).

172 *Reishit Chochmah, Sha'ar HaKedushah* 3 as translated by Yaakov-Shmuel Levinson, *The Jewish Guide to Natural Nutrition* (Nauet, NY: Feldheim Publishers, 1995), 140.

173 Genesis 2:17.

174 Genesis 25:29–34.

175 Numbers 11:4–35.

176 Levinson, *The Jewish Guide to Natural Nutrition*, 129–130.

177 Genesis 7:2. Also see Genesis 7:8.

178 Rashi on Genesis 7:1. Rashi even concludes that we learn from this "that Noah learned Torah." Rabbi Yisrael Isser Zvi Herczeg, *The Torah: With Rashi's Commentary Translated, Annotated, and Elucidated* (Brooklyn, NY: Mesorah Publications, 1999), 72.

179　"Why did the Holy One, blessed be he, order more clean animals [to be saved] than unclean ones? Surely because he desires that offerings should be made to him of the former" *Genesis Rabbah* 26:1. "This division cannot be referring to criteria of human consumption after the flood, when man was permitted to eat flesh, for no such distinction is made in 9:2–3. The categories refer only to suitability for sacrifice." (Nahum Sarna, *The JPS Torah Commentary: Genesis* [New York: Jewish Publication Society, 1989], 54).

180　Rabbi Samson Raphael Hirsch, *The Pentateuch* (6 vols.; Gateshead, Scotland: Judaica Press, 1999), 1:146–147.

181　Rabbi Hirsch, *The Pentateuch*, 1: 37.

182　E.g., Leviticus 3:17, 7:26, 17:12–14, 19:26; Deuteronomy 12:16–27, 15:23. See Sarna, *The JPS Torah Commentary: Genesis*, 54. While Rebbe Nachman would certainly have adhered to the Talmudic interpretation of Genesis 9:3, it is interesting that in his *Likkutei Halachot* he interprets it on a *p'shat* level: "Thus, from Noah's time onward mankind was permitted to eat meat—as long as the animal had undergone kosher slaughter, which brings about a rectification" (*Rebbe Nachamn's Torah: Genesis* [Y. Hall ed.; New York, NY: Breslov Research Institute, 2011], 143).

183　Rabbi Yoel Schwartz, "Noahide Commandments," in *Service from the Heart* (ed. Rabbi Michael Katz et al.; Rose, OK: Oklahoma B'nai Noah Society, 2007), 268. The sages did debate over the specifics of this prohibition: "R Hanania b. Gamaliel said: '[They were also commanded] not to partake of the blood drawn from a living animal.' Our Rabbis taught: '"But flesh with the life thereof, which is the blood thereof, shall ye not eat (Genesis 9:4)," this prohibits flesh cut from the living animal.' R. Hanina b. Gamaliel said: 'It also prohibits blood drawn from a living animal.' What is his reason?—He reads the verse thus: 'flesh with the life thereof [shall ye not eat]:' blood with the life thereof shall ye not eat. But the Rabbis maintain that this reading teaches that flesh cut from live reptiles is permitted. Similarly it is said, 'Only be sure that thou eat not the blood: for the blood is the life,' and thou mayest not eat the life with the flesh (Deuteronomy 12:23). But the Rabbis maintain that the verse teaches that the blood of arteries, with which life goes out, [is also forbidden as blood]" (b.*Sanhedrin* 59a). Rabbi Yehudah argues that the prohibition of *gid hanasheh* (גיד הנשה; Genesis 32:32) applies to Noachides as well because it applied before the Torah was given at Mount Sinai; however, the sages disagree with him (b.*Chullin* 90a).

184　Rabbi Schwartz, "Noahide Commandments," 268. For a full discussion of this commandment see Chaim Clorfene and Yakov Rogalsky, *The Path of the Righteous Gentile* (Southfield, MI: Targum press, 1987), 96–100; Rabbi Yirmeyahu Bindman, *The Seven Colors of the Rainbow:*

*Torah Ethics for Non-Jews* (Colorado Springs, CO: Schueller House, 1995), 104–112; Lichtenstein, *The Seven Laws of Noah*, 53–58 and Rabbi Moshe Weiner, *The Divine Code* (Jerusalem, Israel: Ask Noah International, 2011), 291–367.

185   "It is prohibited to eat meat that has been cut or torn off from a living creature, even a dead animal, if the flesh was cut off when the animal was still alive or when it was on the verge of dying and not slaughtered according to Jewish law. If it was slaughtered by a Jew according to Jewish law, many of its parts are considered to have been cut from a living animal and are therefore forbidden. This refers to all parts that are attached to the trachea and the esophagus and includes the lungs, liver, stomach, and intestines. There are various methods used for killing the animals that are intended for human consumption. Some of them present no problem, but others would call into question the permissibility of eating the above-mentioned organs. One should therefore either not eat those organs, verify that the method which was used to kill the animal was not by cutting its neck, or (and this is the most practical suggestion) only purchase the meat of such organs if it has been slaughtered by a Jew according to Jewish law, i.e., that it is certified kosher. Nearly all the meat for human consumption today comes from animals that have been killed for eating. However some slaughter houses detach parts of the body before the animal has stopped flexing its limbs. If a Noachide is not sure about the source of the meat, it is advised that he buy meat from a person whom he can trust such as a fellow Noachide. In order to remove all doubt, it is possible to buy kosher meat with a kosher label from a recognized rabbinical organization. These rules of flesh from the living hold only towards animals and birds that have warm blood. It does not hold towards reptiles, creeping creatures and fish" (Rabbi Schwartz, "Noahide Commandments," 270–271).

186   Chaim Clorfene and Yakov Rogalsky, *The Path of the Righteous Gentile* (Southfield, MI: Targum press, 1987), 97.

187   Rabbi Bindman, *The Seven Colors of the Rainbow*, 104.

188   Exodus 12:38. Ibn Ezra also connects the "rabble" mentioned in Numbers 11:4 to the "mixed multitude" of the Exodus.

189   E.g., Exodus 23:12; Leviticus 19:10, 23:22, 25:6, 25:47–49.

190   Deuteronomy 24:14–15.

191   There was the additional category of the *ger toshav* ("resident alien," גר תושב), a Gentile who lived among ancient Israel in their nation and was under Israel's legal protection, which included receiving charity if necessary. According to the *Talmud,* they were required to make a formal proclamation renouncing idolatry before a Jewish court of law (*beit din,* בית דין) and then, according to one opinion, to keep all

of the 613 commandments of the Torah with the exception of the prohibition to eat a *neveilah* (נבלה), i.e., an animal that has died of itself (b.*Avodah Zarah* 64b). The Talmud allows the *ger toshav* to eat *neveilah* because Deuteronomy 14:21 forbids an Israelite to eat the carcass of an animal that dies of itself, but it permits the Israelite to give it to a *ger* ("stranger," גר). There also appears to be a less formal type of *ger toshav* who does not make a formal declaration before a *beit din* and therefore is not legally eligible for protection and support (b.*Avodah Zarah* 65a).

192  See Aaron Eby, Toby Janicki, Daniel Lancaster, and Boaz Michael, "Divine Invitation: An Apostolic Call to Torah," 51–54 [Cited 11 February 2011]. Online: http://ffoz.org/_php/download. php?file=Divine_Invitation.pdf.

193  Ancient Judaism viewed the "foreigner" in this passage as not referring to a convert but rather to the *ger toshav* (b.*Yevamot* 48b).

194  This is the reading of the Eastern text which is widely regarded as the more authentic reading. The Western text has instead the prohibitions of "idol offering, blood, and unchastity," where "blood" is interpreted by most in this context to refer to "bloodshed." This would correspond to the three cardinal sins in Judaism: idolatry, illicit sexual relations, and bloodshed. However, many in the West still widely abstained from blood based on Genesis 9:4–6. See Peter J. Thompson, *Paul and the Jewish Law: Halakha in the Letters of the Apostle to the Gentiles* (Minneapolis, MN: Fortress Press, 1990), 179.

195  David Flusser, *Judaism and the Origins of Christianity* (Jerusalem, Israel: The Magnes Press, 1988), 630. Rabbi Shim'on ben Tzemach Duran (14th–15th century) also held this view and argued that the unmentioned Noachide laws were either implied or already being observed. See Aaron Eby, "Rashbatz and the New Testament." *Messiah Journal* 103 (Spring 2010/5770): 58–62.

196  Matthew 16:19. For a good discussion explaining the halachic background to the text see *Torah Club Volume Four: The Chronicles of Messiah*.

197  Richard Bauckham ed., *The Book of Acts in its First Century Setting, Volume 4: Palestinian Setting* (Grand Rapids, MI: Eerdmans, 1995), 425.

198  Many scholars have puzzled over why only one of the four requirements is not a dietary law. This has led to some speculation that *porneia* ("sexual immorality," πορνεία) may have originally meant something else in this context. At least one scholar has suggested emending *porneia* to *porkeia* ("food made of pork," πορκεια), thereby making all of the prohibitions dietary in nature. See H. H. Johnson,

"The Acts, XV. 29," *The Classical Review* 33:5/6 (August/September 1919): 100–101.

199  See also Revelation 2:14, 20.

200  Tomson, *Paul and the Jewish Law*, 180–181.

201  Polhill, *The New American Commentary: Acts*, 330.

202  Oskar Skarsaune, *In the Shadow of the Temple* (Downers Grove, IL: InterVarsity Press, 2002), 239.

203  Chris A. Miller, "Did Peter's Vision in Acts 10 Pertain to Men or the Menu?" *Bibliotheca Sacra* 159:635 (2002): 302–317.

204  Michelle Murray, *Playing a Jewish Game: Gentile Christian Judaizing in the First and Second Centuries CE* (Ontario, Canada: Wilfrid Laurier University Press, 2004), 62.

205  Matthew 8:28–34.

206  m.*Bava Kamma* 7:7.

207  Matthew 13:47–50.

208  *Mishneh Torah, Melachim* 10:9.

209  Rabbi Moshe Weiner, *The Divine Code*, 74.

210  Lauren F Winner, *Mudhouse Sabbath: An Invitation to Spiritual Discipline* (Brewster, MA: Paraclete Press, 2010), 17.